W9-CNE-778

RECOVERING

FROM DIVORCE

Overcoming the
DEATH OF A DREAM

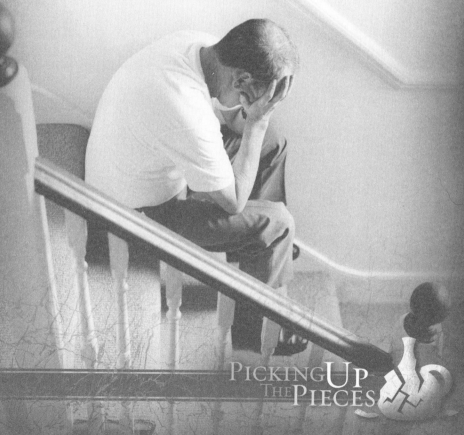

PICKINGUP
THEPIECES

by Ramon Presson

Recovering from Divorce: Overcoming the Death of a Dream
© 2006 Serendipity House

Published by Serendipity House Publishers
Nashville, Tennessee

All rights reserved. No part of this work may be reproduced, stored in a retrieval system, or transmitted in any form or by any means, electronic or mechanical, including photo-copying and recording, without express written permission of the publisher. Requests for permission should be addressed to Serendipity House, 117 10th Avenue North, Nashville, TN 37234.

ISBN: 1-5749-4222-0

Dewey Decimal Classification: 306.89
Subject Headings: DIVORCE

Unless otherwise indicated, all Scripture quotations are taken from the
Holman Christian Standard Bible®,
Copyright © 1999, 2000, 2002, 2003 by Holman Bible Publishers. Used by permission.

Scriptures marked NASB are taken from the *New American Standard Bible®*,
Copyright © 1960, 1962, 1963, 1968, 1971, 1972, 1973, 1975, 1977, 1995 by the
Lockman Foundation. Used by permission. (www.lockman.org)

Scriptures marked NIV are taken from the *Holy Bible, New International Version,* Copyright
© 1973, 1978, 1984 by International Bible Society. Used by permission.

To purchase additional copies of this resource or other studies:
ORDER ONLINE at www.SerendipityHouse.com;
WRITE Serendipity House, 117 10th Avenue North, Nashville, TN 37234
FAX (615) 277-8181
PHONE (800) 525-9563

1-800-525-9563
www.SerendipityHouse.com

Printed in the United States of America

12 11 10 09 08 07 06   1 2 3 4 5 6 7 8 9 10

CONTENTS

Group Meeting Structure

Each of your group meetings will include a four-part agenda.

1. Breaking the Ice:

This section includes fun, uplifting questions to warm up the group and help group members get to know one another better, as they begin the journey of becoming a connected community. These questions prepare the group for meaningful discussion throughout the session.

2. Discovering the Truth:

The heart of each session is the interactive Bible study time. The goal is for the group to discover biblical truths through open, discovery questions that lead to further investigation. The emphasis in this section is two-fold: (1) to provide instruction about the process of recovery and freedom; and (2) understand what the Bible says through interaction within your group.

NOTE: To help the group experience a greater sense of community, it is important for everybody to participate in the "Discovering the Truth" and "Embracing the Truth" discussions. Even though people in a group have differing levels of biblical knowledge, it is vital that group members encourage each other share what they are observing, thinking, and feeling about the Bible passages.

3. Embracing the Truth:

All study should direct group members to action and life change. This section continues the Bible study time, but with an emphasis on leading group members toward integrating the truths they have discovered into their lives. The questions are very practical and application-focused.

4. Connecting:

One of the key goals of this study to lead group members to grow closer to one another as the group develops a sense of community. This section focuses on further application, as well as opportunities for encouraging, supporting, and praying for one another.

Taking it Home:

Between each session, there is some homework for group members. This includes a question to take to God and a question to take to your heart, as well as a few questions to help you prepare for the next session. These experiences are a critical part of your healing process.

The Death of a Dream!

None of us got married with the hope of heartbreaks, shattered dreams, and divorce court. Sure, lots of people end up in divorce, _but this was never supposed to happen in our life, in our marriage!_ Divorce is what happens to other people who don't love each other. Being a part of a divorce recovery group is the last place we ever wanted be. We never anticipated that the word "divorce" and our names would be used in the same sentence, and now we can identify with Job when he says, "The very thing I feared has come upon me," meaning, "The very thing I never imagined possible has crashed into my life."

It's no exaggeration to refer to divorce as a "death." When two people are joined in marriage, they become one, physically, emotionally, and spiritually. Divorce rips apart that fabric of two people that have become one. Both people are deeply hurt, and that hurt extends beyond the couple to friends, to family, especially to our children, and even to a struggling culture that looks desperately for stability, permanence, and relational models. _Divorce is truly the death of a dream—a death of what could have and should have been_. Nobody walks away unscathed. Our fairy tale dies, and our hearts often die with it.

Because divorce is nothing short of a death, there is grieving with a whole host of emotions and struggles. _Recovering From Divorce_ will walk you through the experiences, feelings, and struggles that are common to divorce. God created marriage to be a lifelong relationship, and His heart aches for the pain you're going through. He wants to guide you to a place of hope where He can rebuild the pieces of your broken life. Together with others who are going through the agonies of divorce, you'll explore these topics:

- The Upheaval of Loss
- Breaking Through the Fog of Depression
- Closing the Jaws of Anger
- Experiencing the Freedom of Forgiveness
- Rising from the Paralysis of Worry
- Redeeming the Cost of Your Suffering
- Loneliness and New Relationships
- Finding a New Path to Contentment

Healing always occurs best within a caring community. God invites us to take the journey through our grief together so He can redeem our tears and help us to embrace hope and life again.

Recovering From Divorce is designed to work as a stand alone divorce recovery resource, or as a follow-up study for DivorceCare® groups that want to continue meeting as groups.

UNDERSTANDING THE UPHEAVAL OF LOSS

BREAKING THE ICE - 15 MINUTES

> LEADER: *Be sure to read the introductory material in the front of this book and the Leader's material at the end of the book before this first session. Encourage everyone to answer the "Breaking the Ice" questions. These provide a great way to begin to get to know each other, and to get everyone talking. You should introduce yourself first for question 1.*

1. Take turns introducing yourselves to the group. Tell the group your name and what your favorite hobby is.

2. What was your favorite toy, doll, game, or item you had as a child? Why was that particular item so special to you?

3. Name an item that you lost or misplaced that you wish you could recover just because of its sentimental value.

OPENING PRAYER

God, everyone has lost or tossed away items that we wish we had kept or wish we could find. Thank you for joining us in our journey of healing and rebuilding.

Upheaval

Let's admit it right up front. This is the last kind of group that you ever wanted to be a part of. Divorce is what happens to other people. We never anticipated that the word "divorce" and our names would be used in the same sentence, and now we can identify with Job when he says, "The very thing I feared has come upon me." That can be interpreted as, "The very thing I never imagined possible has come upon me." Well, here we are – not wanting to be here, but needing to be here because we need to heal.

Recovering From Divorce will walk us through the experiences, feelings, and struggles that are common to divorce. It will guide us to a place of hope where God can rebuild our foundations and restore our lives. And we'll travel this journey together because healing always occurs best within a caring community.

In this session, we will: (1) unpack and acknowledge the many implications of the upheaval of divorce; (2) examine the multiple losses within the large loss; and (3) unveil a means to measure our progress in the journey.

Objectives For This Session:
- Recognize the realities of a significant loss
- Begin to accept the implications of your significant loss
- Prepare to move forward together on a healing journey

Discovering The Truth - 30 Minutes

LEADER: Explain that in each session there is a "Discovering the Truth" section that provides understanding of the healing journey and opportunities to discover what the Bible has to say about the topic of the week. Be sure to leave time for the "Embracing the Truth" and "Connecting" segments that follow. Read the explanations between the questions for the group.

The Pain of Loss

Most of us can name toys, baseball cards, dolls, photos, and mementos that we wish we would have kept because of their value today. How were you supposed to know that your Scooby-Doo lunchbox would become a collector's item? Many of us have also lost or misplaced things that were special to us.

The losses involved in divorce are many and painful. The necessary grief that you may be experiencing is legitimate and should not be minimized or rushed. Over the next several weeks we'll explore the issues and needs common to the divorce experience as we move together toward healing and rebuilding our lives.

1. Just as each person's loss is unique, the way each handles that loss will vary as well. Which of the following topics are you currently struggling with? Check all that apply, and share two with your group.
   - ❏ Depression
   - ❏ Forgiveness
   - ❏ Loneliness
   - ❏ Understanding why God let this happen
   - ❏ Anger
   - ❏ Worry/Anxiety
   - ❏ Believing there is hope for future happiness
   - ❏ Other: _____

2. There are a number of losses that accompany the divorce experience. Which of the following losses can you identify with? Check all that apply.
   - ❏ Loss of companionship
   - ❏ Loss of being loved
   - ❏ Loss of physical intimacy
   - ❏ Loss of relationship with spouse's family
   - ❏ Loss of home
   - ❏ Loss of friends
   - ❏ Loss of daily presence of child(ren)
   - ❏ Loss of financial security
   - ❏ Loss of a dream (growing old together, traveling together, spoiling grandchildren together, etc.)
   - ❏ Loss of routines and rituals
   - ❏ Loss of meaningful moments and couple/family traditions
   - ❏ Loss of self-confidence and/or self-esteem
   - ❏ Other: _____

3. Which loss is the hardest for you to deal with? What emotions bubble up when you think of that particular loss?

JOB'S APPROACH TO LOSS

Many people in the Bible experienced and expressed the grief of loss. Few, if any, experienced a loss of the magnitude that Job suffered. Job's loss is not a divorce. In fact, Job's wife was one of the few survivors of his tragic tale. However, Job experienced the total loss of family life as he knew it. In an instant, his entire world grew very dark.

LEADER: Ask various members to read Bible passages when they appear during the session. Encourage individuals to respond to the questions as they feel comfortable. Some group members may want to speak up, while others may wish to remain quiet on certain questions. Strive for participation across the group rather than allowing one or two to carry the discussion.

---

¹³ One day when Job's sons and daughters were eating and drinking wine in their oldest brother's house, ¹⁴ a messenger came to Job and reported: "While the oxen were plowing and the donkeys grazing nearby, ¹⁵ the Sabeans swooped down and took them away. They struck down the servants with the sword, and I alone have escaped to tell you!"

¹⁶ He was still speaking when another messenger came and reported: "A lightning storm struck from heaven. It burned up the sheep and the servants, and devoured them, and I alone have escaped to tell you!" ¹⁷ That messenger was still speaking when yet another came and reported: "The Chaldeans formed three bands, made a raid on the camels, and took them away. They struck down the servants with the sword, and I alone have escaped to tell you!"

¹⁸ He was still speaking when another messenger came and reported: "Your sons and daughters were eating and drinking wine in their oldest brother's house. ¹⁹ Suddenly a powerful wind swept in from the desert and struck the four corners of the house. It collapsed on the young people so that they died, and I alone have escaped to tell you!"

²⁰ Then Job stood up, tore his robe and shaved his head. He fell to the ground and worshiped, ²¹ saying: Naked I came from my mother's womb, and naked I will leave this life. The LORD gives, and the LORD takes away. Praise the name of the LORD.

²² Throughout all this Job did not sin or blame God for anything.

JOB 1:13-22 (HCSB)

4. What losses does Job experience?

5. If you were Job how would you be feeling about life? About God?

6. How does Job respond to his losses? How do you think you might have responded? Was Job's reaction normal in this situation? If you said yes, why do you think it is? Explain your answer.

We might be inclined to say that Job exhibits a lack of grief concerning his loss or that his response is borne out of shock and denial. However, Job's immediate tearing of his robe and shaving of his head is his expression of profound mourning. This response is a customary and physical expression commonly found in the Bible. Furthermore, just because the text does not describe Job as weeping or sobbing does not mean that he did not do so. He very likely sobbed himself into exhaustion.

In the end, Job does not blame God for his profound loss. However, don't think that genuinely spiritual people never wrestled with God. Take note of the raw honesty of these hurting people from the Scriptures:

JOB
I will not restrain my mouth. I will speak in the anguish of my spirit; I will complain in the bitterness of my soul. ... I prefer strangling, death rather than life in this body.

JOB 7:11,15 (HCSB)

DAVID
I have sunk in deep mud, and there is no footing; I have come into deep waters, and a flood sweeps over me. I am weary from my crying; my throat is parched. My eyes fail, looking for my God.

PSALM 69:2-3 (HCSB)

JEREMIAH
Why has my pain become unending, my wound incurable, refusing to be healed? You truly have become like a mirage to me—water that is not reliable.

JEREMIAH 15:18 (HCSB)

GIDEON
If the LORD is with us, why has all this happened? And where are all His wonders that our fathers told us about?

JUDGES 6: 13A (HCSB)

JESUS
My God, My God, why have You forsaken Me?

MATTHEW 27:46 (HCSB)

7. What encouragement or reassurance do you take from the honest statements of these heroes of the faith?

8. Describe the feelings you've had toward God in the midst of your divorce.

EMBRACING THE TRUTH – 20 MINUTES

LEADER: "Embracing the Truth" is the section in which the group members will begin to integrate the truth they are discovering during the session into their personal lives. Be aware that the level of hurt and response to this hurt will be different for different people, so the rate of life application will vary accordingly.

THE HEALING JOURNEY

As we launch into this journey together, there are a few things to keep in mind about emotional and spiritual healing.

(1) EVERYONE'S HEALING PATH IS UNIQUE AND COMPLEX.

While there are common experiences and almost universal issues that are encountered, your healing journey is unique because ...
- your personality is unique
- your marriage was unique
- your former spouse is unique
- your coping methods are unique
- your divorce drama continues to evolve daily driven by multiple unique factors

Because everyone's experience is unique and complex, we cannot project our past or current experiences onto anyone else in the group. Let's respect each other's story, realizing we will each move through this process at our own pace.

(2) The healing path is seldom a straight, ascending line.

In a purely medical model, physical healing (illness or injury recovery) is frequently a fairly consistent and progressive move toward restored health. This is not the case with emotional healing. In emotional and spiritual healing, there is typically a combination of progress, setbacks, and plateaus involved.

The progression of emotional healing seldom looks like this:

Instead, it typically looks more like this:

This is normal and to be expected.

1. Have you felt like you were on life's emotional rollercoaster? Describe what you felt, and what questions you wanted to ask God during these ups and downs.

Healing and progress can often be measured by your Symptom FDI.

- **F**requency
  Your healing progress can be measured by frequency when you cry less often, break fewer lamps, laugh more often, complete more projects, and are less sarcastic when you talk with your ex-spouse.

- **D**uration
  Your healing can be measured by duration when your crying episodes become shorter in length, and your fits of rage become briefer. You spend less time at private pity parties.

- **I**ntensity
  Your healing can be measured by intensity when your weeping becomes more like silent tears than wailing that wakes the neighbors. Your severe depression gets milder, and you slap pillows instead of punch holes in the walls. You are able to express anger to your ex-spouse without making death threats, or losing your temper.

2. Identify a symptom in your own life that is already showing some improvement. Is the progress evident in frequency, duration, or intensity? How can you tell?

3. Is there any symptom in which you feel stuck? Is there any symptom currently worsening? Explain.

If you have areas that are stuck or worsening don't panic. Remember that the healing journey includes plateaus where progress seems to hit the PAUSE button and setbacks where you bottom out. Although we would like our healing to be a straight, ascending line, we must learn to accept and embrace the wild rollercoaster ride as normal.

CONNECTING – 25 MINUTES

LEADER: Use the "Connecting" time to help the group members bond. The invitation during this session is for people to become comfortable opening up within the group. You will find with divorced adults that it is not difficult to get them to open up and share their stories or feelings. You may, however, have to intervene on occasion to prevent the sharing time from degrading into an ex-spouse bashing session.

This "Connecting" time acknowledges the mutual experience of loss, and rekindles the hope found in Christ and in community with one another. Encourage people to begin leaning on and supporting each other in prayer and in other tangible ways.

LEADER INSTRUCTIONS FOR GROUP EXPERIENCE:

Pass candles out to everyone in the room. Choose candles that won't drip hot wax onto the person or the host's furniture. Dim the lights. Light a center candle on the floor or table and have everyone light their candles from the center flame. When all of the candles have been lit, have the group take a moment to notice the warmth and the glow of their own flame. DISCUSS QUESTION 1. Then, just before question 2, on your cue, have everyone blow their candles out.

1. If these were candles atop a birthday cake that you were about to blow out, how would you feel? Why would you say that?

The events and emotions are entirely different when your candle has been extinguished by the winds of divorce. (Blow out you candle when instructed by your leader.)

2. What did you see when you blew out your candle? What did you smell? Did you feel anything after everyone extinguished their candles?

3. What did you feel when your marriage was extinguished?

LEADER: *At this time, the group leader should reignite his/her candle from the center candle, which never went out. The leader will use his/her candle to re-light the candle of the group member closest to him/her. One by one, group members will "pass the flame" until all the candles are lit again.*

Once all of the candles are lit, say, "Jesus said, 'I am the light of the world. He who believes in Me will not walk in darkness.' The center candle never went out. From it we brought light and life back to our own candle. We also shared our flame with one another. God gives us Himself, and He gives us the gift of supportive friendships. Over the next several weeks, we'll regain our strength from God and receive support, acceptance, and encouragement from one another."

4. What or whom do you think the center candle represents? What significance did you see in group members passing the flame to relight each others' candles? How does having these other candles surrounding you make you feel?

5. We were designed to live in community, to help and support one another. What's one tangible thing this group could do for you this week? Write it down, and then share it with the group.

Prayer is one the vital ways we can re-connect to the power source, the Holy Spirit of God. It is also a key way we can help each other by inviting God to work in someone's life. How can we pray for you today?

My Prayer Requests:

My Group's Prayer Requests:

In addition to praying for each other's specific needs, let's thank God that we're together and that His light will light our journey. Let's thank God that we'll be support beams holding one another up as we make our way through the complexity of divorce.

TAKING IT HOME

LEADER: Explain that the "Taking It Home" section in each session contains an introspective question to ask of your heart and a question to take to God. In addition, there a few questions to help prepare for the next session. Strongly encourage everyone to complete the activities before the next session. These will greatly enhance both individual and group experiences. Be sure to highlight the importance of journaling thoughts, memories, or key insights that God reveals.

LOOKING INWARD ... QUESTIONS TO TAKE TO MY HEART:

Look into your heart for the answer to these questions. This is introspection time—time to grapple with what drives your thinking and behavior. <u>Every action has a corresponding belief that drives it</u>. Dig for what you believe in the deep recesses of your heart about God, yourself, and the world in which you live. Be sure to capture your thoughts.

✳ Each of us will experience progress, setbacks, and plateaus. How do I feel about my progress thus far? How have I handled my setbacks? Is there a plateau I need to move off of?

✳ What beliefs about myself are driving my response to the divorce?

LOOKING UPWARD ... QUESTIONS TO TAKE TO GOD:

When you ask God a question, expect His Spirit to respond to your heart. Be careful not to rush it, or manufacture an answer. Don't turn the Bible into a reference book or spiritual encyclopedia. Just pose the question to God, and wait on Him. The litmus test for anything we hear from God is alignment with the Bible as our ultimate truth source.

Our beliefs and attitudes about God are very subtle, and often hidden from our immediate awareness. However, what we really believe in our core about God heavily influences not only our experience with God but our entire view of life.

✳ God, what belief/attitude toward You am I holding on to that is preventing me from being as close to You as I could be?

✳ Have I discredited Your love, Your goodness, or Your power because of my divorce? If so, how? How do you feel about me, God?

LOOKING FORWARD ... PREPARE FOR SESSION 2:

NOTE: Be sure to review the Group Covenant in the next page so you're prepared for a brief group discussion at the next meeting.

Capture your thoughts and feelings in the "Breaking Through the Fog Journal" on the next page, as you continue on your healing journey. Consider these Session 2 questions:

1. If my depression was a color it would be:
   - ❏ Light blue – not that bad
   - ❏ Grey – like a cold rainy day
   - ❏ Brown – like leaves that once had color
   - ❏ Black – like darkness that surrounds me
   - ❏ Other: _____

2. If I my depression was weather it would be:
   - ❏ Mostly sunny – some clouds, but generally clear and warm
   - ❏ Overcast – brief moments of sunshine but mostly cloudy
   - ❏ Constant drizzle – keeps me emotionally damp
   - ❏ Scattered thunderstorms – random thunder, lightning strikes, and deluges of rain
   - ❏ Hurricane – severe with damage
   - ❏ Blizzard – I can't see past my discouragement
   - ❏ Ice storm – I'm stuck inside myself with nowhere to go
   - ❏ Other: _____

3. How difficult is it to admit to another person that you feel down or depressed? What makes it difficult?

4. What are your typical methods of coping with or responding to your times of sorrow or depression?

GROUP COVENANT

As you begin this study, it is important that your group covenant together, agreeing to live out important group values. Once these values are agreed upon, your group will be on its way to experiencing true redemptive community. It's very important that your group discuss these values—preferably as you begin this study.

* PRIORITY: While we are in this group, we will give the group meetings priority. All the sessions are integrated, with each session building on the sessions that precede them. Committed attendance is vital to our healing journey together.

  NOTE: Due to the focus of this group on taking the journey through the emotions and losses of divorce, group sessions will require a full 90 minutes to complete, so plan accordingly.

* PARTICIPATION AND FAIRNESS: Because we are here to receive help, we commit to participation and interaction in the group. No one dominates. We will be fair to others and concentrate on telling our own stories briefly.

* HOMEWORK: Homework experiences are an integral and vital part of the recovery process. Assignments between each session include: (1) A Question to Take to My Heart; (2) A Question to Take to God; (3) Thoughts to journal to prepare for the next session.

* RESPECT AND OWNERSHIP: Everyone is given the right to his or her own opinions, and all questions are encouraged and respected. We will not judge or condemn as others share their stories. We are each responsible for our own recovery and will not "own" someone else's. Offensive language is not permitted.

* CONFIDENTIALITY: Anything said in our meetings is never repeated outside the meeting without permission from the group member. This is vital in creating the environment of trust and openness required to facilitate the healing and freedom. Names of attendees will not be shared with others.

* LIFE CHANGE: We will regularly assess our progress and will complete the "Taking it Home" activities to reinforce what we are learning, and to better integrate those lessons into our personal journeys.

* CARE AND SUPPORT: Permission is given to call upon each other at any time, especially in times of crisis. The group will provide care for every member.

* ACCOUNTABILITY AND INTEGRITY: We agree to let the members of our group hold us accountable to commitments we make in whatever loving ways we decide upon. Unsolicited advice-giving is not permitted. We will build a close relationship with an accountability partner for mutual growth and responsibility. Men will help men and women will help to women in order to uphold the spirit of integrity. No dating within the group!

* EXPECTATIONS OF FACILITATORS: This meeting is not professional therapy. We are not licensed therapists. Group facilitators are volunteers whose only desire is to encourage people in finding freedom and hope.

I agree to all of the above_____ date: _____

BREAKING THROUGH THE FOG JOURNAL

BREAKING THROUGH THE FOG OF DEPRESSION

BREAKING THE ICE – 20 MINUTES

> LEADER: The "Breaking the Ice" questions will help group members get better acquainted and begin talking casually about the session topic. Keep the tone of the conversation light and fun. Be sure everyone gets a turn to talk.

1. We were all intrigued by Superman's x-ray vision when we were growing up. When you were a kid, what did you wish you could see through, and what did you want to see?
   - ❏ The wall between my room and my brother's or sister's room. I still think he/she got to stay up later than me.
   - ❏ The teacher's desk. I needed the answers to most of my tests.
   - ❏ My dad's pockets. I knew he had enough change to buy me an ice cream cone!
   - ❏ Wrapped Christmas gifts; the suspense just killed me.
   - ❏ Other: _____

2. Which of the movies below best describes the way you feel about your life today?
   - ❏ *Groundhog Day* – I'm beginning to wonder if I know how to do life right.
   - ❏ *Castaway* – I feel like I'm all alone without the tools to cope.
   - ❏ *Gone With the Wind* – I'd do almost anything to survive.
   - ❏ *Matrix* – Surely there's another reality where I have some power.
   - ❏ *Braveheart* – I'm beginning to believe there's a hero coming to save me.
   - ❏ Other: _____

In the first session we talked about the upheaval caused by divorce and the multiple layers of loss. We noted that one way that healing can be measured is by progress in Symptom FDI (Frequency, Duration, Intensity). As God brings healing and growth, we'll likely see evidence of improvement in the frequency, duration, and intensity of key symptoms.

3. How did your "Taking It Home" assignments go? What did you hear from God about His feelings for you? Were you surprised either by god's response or by your beliefs deep down inside?

4. What emotions or thoughts are you wrestling with after pondering these homework questions about depression?

5. Did anything happen with your ex-spouse or with your children this week that reminded you about some part of last week's session, or your homework questions?

Opening Prayer

Holy Spirit, please join us in our session today. Sometimes it feels as though our joy has been stolen, ripped off by some thieving intruder. Our joy is gone, and we don't expect to ever see it again. Lord, help us to grieve, but not as people who have no hope. Help us to lean into our pain without falling over the rail. Help us track down and capture the joy thief and recover reasons to smile and excuses to laugh.

Rebuilding After the Storm

In Session 1 we began our journey together towards healing from divorce. Author David Sittser, in reflecting upon the loss of his family in a tragic car accident, realized that he would never "get over" his devastating loss. He said that their deaths would become a part of him like decaying matter becomes assimilated into the soil. The event would not always overwhelm him or permanently immobilize him, but it would always be a part of him. It would not define him, but it would always impact him. For him to expect otherwise was naïve thinking or spiritual denial.

Likewise, you will never completely overcome your divorce. It's like a tornado that has left a wide swath of damage and storm ravaged areas that need to be rebuilt. With God's help, you too will rebuild. Healing is a process, and we're in this together. In today's session, we'll talk about breaking through the fog of depression.

Objectives For This Session:
- Recognize the symptoms of depression
- Understand the causes of depression
- Learn to break free from depression's hold

DISCOVERING THE TRUTH – 30 MINUTES

LEADER: *Read the questions and explanations between questions for the group. Encourage every-one to participate in responding to the questions, but keep things moving. Ask for volunteers to read the Bible verses. Be sure to leave time for "Embracing the Truth" and "Connecting" coming segments.*

MODEL HEROES?

Do you think the heroes of the Bible were always positive, upbeat people who never let anything get them down? Think again. Listen to Jeremiah in Lamentations 3:19-20:

I remember my affliction and my wandering, the bitterness and the gall. I well remember them, and my soul is downcast within me. (NIV)

Let's read it now in a contemporary paraphrase:

I'll never forget the trouble, the utter lostness, the taste of ashes, the poison I've swallowed. I remem-ber it all—oh, how well I remember—the feeling of hitting the bottom. (The Message)

1. Jeremiah doesn't use the term depression here, so what about his words and tone tells you that he is indeed experiencing a level of depression?

2. What significance do you find in Jeremiah using the phrase "I remember" twice?

3. How does what we choose to focus on, and practice remembering (replaying in our minds) contribute to our depression?

(NOTE: We are only asking about memories that contribute to depression. We are not insinuating that you should work towards some type of amnesia about the past.)

4. Is there an idea, image, ideal, or memory that you frequently rewind and replay on your mental screen? Describe the power of it when you press "Play." How would you describe your emotions when you replay that experience?

THE WARNING SIGNS

There are well-documented symptoms that accompany depression. These symptoms warn of the onset of depression and indicate its severity.

One symptom is a *diminished energy* level. Your *sleep* is usually altered. Either you cannot sleep, or you want to sleep all the time. Your normal *appetite* may also be disturbed. You will either have no appetite or eat more than usual. This symptom gives a whole new meaning to the phrase "comfort food." Your *concentration* is impaired, and you will frequently become more *irritable*. While you're depressed, completing simple tasks will seem like major undertakings. Your *interest* in previously enjoyed activities may drop, and your *self-confidence* may suffer a major blow. During a depression, *apathy* usually replaces motivation. Finally, depression *hides the view of a hopeful future* and can even cause you to wish for your death or, worse yet, contemplate suicide.

5. Which of the above indicators do you readily identify with? Don't be surprised or alarmed if you identify with several or even most of them, especially after what you've been through.

JEREMIAH'S HOPE

LEADER: The questions that follow will help people to understand Jeremiah's and David's perspectives on depression. At times, there are related personal application questions. However, most of the application questions appear in the "Embracing the Truth" section. Invite volunteers to read the various Scripture passages as you come to them.

Let's return to Jeremiah and the passage in Lamentations:

²¹ *Yet this I call to mind and therefore I have hope:* ²² *Because of the* LORD's *great love we are not consumed, for his compassions never fail.* ²³ *They are new every morning; great is Your faithfulness.* ²⁴ *I say to myself, 'The* LORD *is my portion; therefore I will wait for Him.* ²⁵ *The* LORD *is good to those whose hope is in Him, to the one who seeks Him;* ²⁶ *it is good to wait quietly for the salvation of the* LORD.

LAMENTATIONS 3:21-26 (NIV)

The word "salvation" in the Old Testament is synonymous with "deliverance." Old Testament writers spoke of salvation as being help from the LORD in this present life, compared to our present use of salvation, which usually connotes eternal life in heaven.

Read the same verses from *The Message*:

²¹ *But there's one other thing I remember, and remembering, I keep a grip on hope:* ²² GOD's *loyal love couldn't have run out, His merciful love couldn't have dried up.* ²³ *They're created new every morning. How great Your faithfulness!* ²⁴ *I'm sticking with* GOD *(I say it over and over). He's all I've got left.* ²⁵ GOD *proves to be good to the man who passionately waits, to the woman who diligently seeks.* ²⁶ *It's a good thing to quietly hope, quietly hope for help from* GOD.

6. What words or phrases from this section of Lamentations most capture your attention? Why do you believe those passages connect with you at this time in your life?

7. Note the similarity between "I call this to mind" (verse 21) and "I say to myself" (verse 24). What lesson is Jeremiah subtly communicating to us?

8. Hope is either wishful thinking or based solidly in some reality or promise. What does this passage say to you about legitimate hope?

Hope is a critical component when it comes to dealing with depression. For someone suffocating under depression, hope is oxygen. We cannot live without hope. Yet, the deceptive voice of depression seeks to convince us of two things.

(1) There is no reason to hope. Depression tells us that hoping is a waste of time and energy because nothing will change.

(2) Depression tries to convince us that there is nothing promising to hope for. Since you can't get your marriage back, save it and improve it, what else matters? Depression tells you that divorce has fatally frostbitten your flowers, and is preventing spring from ever coming.

DAVID'S PRAYER

Read David's plea to God. Let these words be your own prayer for deliverance from depression's gravitational pull.

> LEADER: *Give group members a couple of minutes to silently pray this prayer to God.*

[14] *Rescue me from the mire, do not let me sink; deliver me from those who hate me, from the deep waters.* [15] *Do not let the flood waters engulf me or the depths swallow me up or the pit close its mouth over me.* [16] *Answer me, O LORD, out of the goodness of your love; in your great mercy turn to me.* [17] *Do not hide your face from your servant; answer me quickly, for I am in trouble.* [18] *Come near and rescue me ...*

PSALM 69:14-18 (NIV)

EMBRACING THE TRUTH – 25 MINUTES

We must understand that a certain level of depression is normal and expected in the face of a profound loss like divorce. We don't want to take up residence and stay stuck in a depression, but we need to realize that it's one of the venues we'll pass through on our journey toward healing.

The problem is that depression tends to generate behaviors that further compound our problems. In order for healing to occur, we must be in authentic relationships with other people who can:

- Encourage and guide us on this journey
- Incorporate raw and honest prayer,
- Provide balanced biblical thinking
- Unleash positive action into our daily lives

1. What do the raw and honest feelings expressed by several biblical writers communicate to you personally? On a scale of 1 to 10, how well have you done at being as honest and intense in crying out to God?

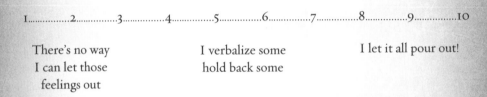

1...........2...........3...........4...........5...........6...........7...........8...........9...........10

There's no way   I verbalize some   I let it all pour out!
I can let those   hold back some
  feelings out

2. After he describes his downcast soul and declares that he's hit bottom, Jeremiah proclaims, "Yet this I call to mind and therefore I have hope." What do you need to "call to mind" or remember?

3. Jeremiah writes, "I say to myself ..." What reassuring truths do you need to say to yourself in the midst of depression?

4. Which of these counter-productive behaviors can you identify with?
   Check all that apply.
   ❏ Isolation – I isolate myself and avoid people
   ❏ Eating – I overeat or neglect to fuel my body with good nutrition
   ❏ Disconnection – I cease activities that I previously enjoyed
   ❏ Laziness – I give in to lethargy and avoid exercise
   ❏ Shopping – I spend money as a form of medication
   ❏ Sleep Deprivation – I stay up too late watching TV and don't get enough rest
   ❏ Self-Medication – I dull the pain with alcohol or some other substance
   ❏ Promiscuity – I attempt to cure depression and loneliness with sexual activity
   ❏ Other: _____

5. What are some healthy countermeasures to the behaviors in question 4 that we can
   agree to put into action together? What are some reasonable beginning steps that you
   can take in the next few weeks?

Paul writes:

*We are pressed on every side by troubles, but we are not crushed and broken. We are perplexed, but
we don't give up and quit. We are hunted down, but God never abandons us. We get knocked down,
but we get up again and keep going.*

2 CORINTHIANS 4:8-9 (THE LIVING BIBLE)

Notice that Paul acknowledges the reality of personal pain in four distinct phrases. Yet,
for every pain mentioned, Paul provides a truth to recall and cling to.

6. Look closely at Paul's statements in 2 Corinthians 4:8-9. What words or phrases hold
   special meaning for you? Why?

CONNECTING – 15 MINUTES

LEADER: Use this "Connecting" time to develop more closeness within your group, as well as to encourage and support one another in practical ways throughout the week. Invite everyone to join in and to be open and supportive with each other.

LEADER INSTRUCTIONS FOR GROUP EXPERIENCE: Have the TV/DVD player set up close by, and the Castaway *DVD cued up to the scene where Tom Hank's character loses Wilson in the ocean. Show Scene 24 from 1:40:33 to 1:45:57 minutes on the DVD. Verbally set the scene by reading the line that precedes question 1.*

In the movie *Castaway*, Tom Hank's character is the sole survivor of a plane crash at sea. He is stranded alone on an island for several years. With no person to talk to, he fashions a friend, that he calls Wilson, out of a volleyball. In this scene, Tom Hanks loses Wilson in the ocean.

1. In your opinion, why is this scene of a man losing a $12 dollar volleyball so emotionally gripping? Why do you think it affects you the way it does?

2. How does the profound grief of losing a beloved volleyball translate into the loss within your own story?

3. How can this group support you practically this week as you ask God to help you understand how to cope with the intense emotions from your loss? How can we pray for you today?

My Prayer Requests:

My Group's Prayer Requests:

In addition to specific prayer requests, pray together for each person individually, to begin to see Jesus as the Deliverer in whom he or she can place hope in the midst of despair.

Taking It Home

Mark an X on each scale that represents your current experience of depression according to the FDI of your symptoms:

Frequency _____

              getting worse   staying the same   getting better

Duration _____

              getting worse   staying the same   getting better

Intensity _____

              getting worse   staying the same   getting better

Looking Inward ... A Question to Take to My Heart:

Look into your heart for the answer to these questions. This is introspection time—time to grapple with what drives your thinking and behavior. <u>Every action has a corresponding belief that drives it.</u> Dig for what you believe in the deep recesses of your heart about God, yourself, and the world in which you live. Be sure to capture your thoughts.

* What might may be preventing me from facing my loss or embracing my grief?" Once you have identified an obstacle, discuss it with God. Hand your obstacle off to Him.

Looking Upward ... A Question to Take to God:

When you ask God a question, expect His Spirit to respond to your heart. Be careful not to rush it, or manufacture an answer. Don't jot down your idea of the "right answer." Don't turn the Bible into a reference book or spiritual encyclopedia. Just pose the question to God, and wait on Him to speak personally in a fresh way. The litmus test for anything we hear from God is alignment with the Bible as our ultimate truth source. Always write down what you hear from God.

* God, what self-defeating thoughts and behaviors are holding me captive to depression? Would you help me to distinguish between reasonable depression given my recent circumstances, and harmful depression that's dragging me down?

Looking Forward... Prepare for Session 3:

Please capture your thoughts and feelings in the "My Feelings Journal" on the next page, as you work through your healing process. Consider these questions that will be discussed in Session 3:

1. How would I rate my current level of anger in the midst my divorce situation?

1..............2..............3..............4..............5..............6..............7..............8..............9..............10
  cool   quite warm   simmering   very hot   boiling over

2. How would I rate my current effectiveness in handling my anger?

1..............2..............3..............4..............5..............6..............7..............8..............9..............10
disastrous   ineffective   somewhat effective   very effective

3. What are the ways that am I coping with my pain? In what ways are my current coping skills helping me?

4. In what ways are my current ways of coping with my pain keeping me stuck?

My Feelings Journal

CLOSING THE JAWS OF ANGER

BREAKING THE ICE - 15 MINUTES

> *LEADER: The "Breaking the Ice" questions will help put people at ease and continue to help them connect with each other.*

1. When I was a teenager I was the most angry when …
   - ❏ Someone embarrassed me in public
   - ❏ I couldn't remember the answers for a test I had studied for
   - ❏ My boyfriend or girlfriend broke up with me
   - ❏ A friend betrayed me or broke a trust
   - ❏ A parent or teacher disciplined me for something I didn't do
   - ❏ Other: _____

2. When I'm angry, other people would probably describe me as:
   - ❏ Cold – I give the cold shoulder
   - ❏ Warm – I pretend to be just fine
   - ❏ Simmering – I'm hot but under control
   - ❏ Boiling – I'm ready to explode
   - ❏ Spilling Over – Sometimes I do explode
   - ❏ Other: _____

3. When someone is angry at me, I'm a:
   - ❏ Tennis Racquet – Here comes the anger back at ya, pal!
   - ❏ Sponge – The anger is absorbed and disappears, but I'm soaked inside.
   - ❏ Piston – Too much friction causes me to shut down.
   - ❏ Baseball Glove – I catch the anger and hold it.
   - ❏ Fish Hook – If you bite me, I'll make you wish you hadn't.
   - ❏ Bulletproof Vest – The anger doesn't phase me.
   - ❏ Sandcastle – Anger flattens me like a wave.
   - ❏ Other: _____

4. How did your "Taking It Home" assignments go? Did you discover any obstacles from talking with your heart or with God to facing your lose or embracing your grief? Please explain so you and the group will benefit from your story.

5. As you spent some time thinking about your anger this week, what issue surrounding your divorce surfaced as something that really pushes your anger button? Also, which of your former spouse's behaviors really get you fired up?

OPENING PRAYER

Lord, we confess that we're sometimes consumed by our anger. At other times, we try to stuff it down inside. We don't really know what to do with it. Having anger is like receiving a package of mysterious parts without instructions. It's ours, but we don't really know what it is, how to put it together, or how to use it. We have some preferred ways of dealing with anger, but they really aren't working for us very well. Help us, Holy Spirit, to understand this familiar but unwelcome emotion, and learn better ways to express anger.

BLOWING THE LID OFF

In our last session we explored the emotional experience of depression and realized that a certain level of depression is normal and expected in the face of a loss like divorce. We also discovered that we have a genuine hope that is found in God's faithfulness and profound love for us. We advocated challenging the self-defeating thoughts and behaviors that leave us stuck in the mire of depression. In our session today, we'll take the lid off another powerful emotional experience – anger. We'll acknowledge that a degree of anger is normal and even necessary in the midst of our loss. Finally, we'll seek to understand the anger in us, and develop healthier ways to process and express it.

OBJECTIVES FOR THIS SESSION:

- Understand the underlying roots of anger
- Recognize unhealthy and ungodly expressions of anger
- Identify and practice healthy and godly expressions of anger

DISCOVERING THE TRUTH – 35 MINUTES

LEADER: *Ask someone to read Ephesians 4:25-27, 31-32 aloud. Encourage everyone to participate in responding to the questions. Read the explanations between questions for the group. Be sure to leave ample time for "Embracing the Truth" and "Connecting" segments later in the session.*

THE ROOTS OF ANGER

²⁵ *Therefore, laying aside falsehood, speak the truth each one of you with his neighbor, for we are members of one another.* ²⁶ *Be angry, and yet do not sin; do not let the sun go down on your anger,* ²⁷ *and do not give the devil an opportunity.* ²⁸ *He who steals must steal no longer; but rather he must labor, performing with his own hands what is good, so that he will have something to share with one who has need.* ²⁹ *Let no unwholesome word proceed from your mouth, but only such a word as is good for edification according to the need of the moment, so that it will give grace to those who hear.* ³⁰ *Do not grieve the Holy Spirit of God, by whom you were sealed for the day of redemption.* ³¹ *Let all bitterness and wrath and anger and clamor and slander be put away from you, along with all malice.* ³² *Be kind to one another, tender-hearted, forgiving each other, just as God in Christ also has forgiven you.*

EPHESIANS 4:25-32 (NASB)

1. According to verses 25-26, is our anger wrong? Why would God encourage us to feel and express anger?

When expressed rightly, anger is not always harmful or unloving. Anger in itself is not sinful; rather, it's often what we do when we're angry that is sin. Dr. Les Carter maintains that anger is actually a gift or a tool given to build relationships; however, it's often misused as a device of harm. A hammer in the hand of a carpenter is a tool of construction, but it's a lethal weapon in the possession of madman. Let's deal with anger as an emotion, and as a behavior that can be potentially sinful.

Anger is not a primary emotion. It is typically caused by an underlying thought or feeling. Primary root emotions are (1) hurt or betrayal, and (2) frustration due to due to blockage of our goals. For example, we may feel our character was questioned or attacked, our rights were violated, our authority defied, or something or someone we value was dishonored. These hardly cover the list, but you get the idea – an underlying thought or feeling works its way through the assembly line in our mental factory and comes out in the product of anger.

2. Think of the last time you got really angry with someone. What was the underlying thought or feeling of your anger?

IMPLOSIVE ANGER

Two unhealthy ways of managing anger are (1) to express it aggressively, or (2) to withhold it. Dr. Gary Chapman calls these explosive and implosive anger. Implosive anger is internalized anger that is never expressed. "I'm not angry; I'm just frustrated" or "I'm not mad; I'm just disappointed" are common expressions of an imploder.

3. What are the results of unexpressed or bottled up anger (see Ephesians 4:27-32)?

4. In Ephesians 4:29, the word for "unwholesome" means "rotten." How does anger turn to rottenness?

5. According to Ephesians 4:29-30, what does stuffed anger eventually turn into?

The results of implosive anger are passive-aggressive behavior, displaced anger, physiological and emotional stress, resentment, bitterness, and hatred. Imploders typically keep score, so the potential for a delayed explosion from a dormant volcano is always there.

When Paul advises, "do not let the sun go down on your anger," he's telling us to deal with anger promptly and effectively before it spreads and does more damage. He also warns, "do not give the devil an opportunity." Paul explains that to poorly managed anger is to offer the devil a "*topos*"—a plot of land in our lives. The devil uses that land like a military base from which to launch more attacks into the relationship.

6. Given the way I typically deal with anger, the amount of territory I unwittingly give to the devil is probably comparable to:
   - ❏ A postage stamp
   - ❏ My garage
   - ❏ My front yard
   - ❏ A football field
   - ❏ Africa
   - ❏ Texas
   - ❏ Other: _____

EXPLOSIVE ANGER

Explosive anger is the other unhealthy, ungodly management technique. It is an uncontrolled fury that may manifest in verbal and/or physical abuse. !

7. What is typically the first outcome of all poorly managed anger (see Ephesians 4:31)?

8. How would you define explosive anger? Describe a time you've experienced explosive words or behavior, and how it made you feel.

Explosive anger verbally attacks by screaming, cursing, condemning, name-calling, humiliating, or threatening. It damages self-esteem and trust, and ultimately destroys a relationship when the exploder causes the anger recipient to retreat for emotional safety. Exploders frequently blame their victims for their anger and/or minimize their outbursts by calling them "blowing off steam" or "getting something off my chest." In extreme cases, the exploder may grab, push, or strike in anger. All unhealthy anger is harmful, but physical abuse is intolerable and protective measures should be sought. Don't try to justify or rationalize explosive anger—get rid of it and replace it with healthy approaches!

EMBRACING THE TRUTH – 25 MINUTES

CONSTRUCTIVE ANGER

A healthy and godly way to manage anger is to use it for productive and constructive results. Dr. Les Carter calls this "assertive anger." Assertive anger's goals are to solve the problem and, at the same time, respect the people involved.

1. Which is most true of your style of managing anger?
   - ❏ I hold it in (implosive; stuffer)
   - ❏ I let it fly (explosive; blower)
   - ❏ I express it appropriately (constructive)

2. If God wants to use anger as a tool to resolve problems, while still respecting people, how can we achieve that? As a group, brainstorm ways that we can deal with our anger in productive and constructive ways.

Here are some practical ways to appropriately and constructively express feelings of anger.

(1) Admit to yourself and to God that you are angry.

Remember that the emotion of anger is not sinful; it is the improper expression of it that becomes sin. Don't try to super-spiritualize your anger away. Admit that you're angry. In Genesis 4:6 the LORD asks Cain, "Why are you so angry?" The Scriptures do not indicate that Cain answers or admits his anger.

(2) Restrain your immediate response and locate the root of your anger.

Ephesians 4:29 warns us not to allow rotten talk to spurt out of our mouths. Just because you feel something doesn't mean you have to say it. James 1:19 instructs us to "be slow to anger." Bite your tongue and think before you speak. Ask yourself, "What belief or feeling is producing this anger? What is my perceived injustice?" Don't try to intellectualize your anger away; rather, prepare yourself to speak in a way that will express the true issue beneath that anger.

3. If anger is a response to perceived injustice, which of the following "wrongs" ignite feelings of anger toward your former spouse? Being ...
   ❏ Insulted
   ❏ Manipulated
   ❏ Unappreciated
   ❏ Ignored
   ❏ Humiliated
   ❏ Disrespected
   ❏ Mocked
   ❏ Betrayed
   ❏ Accused
   ❏ Threatened
   ❏ Other: _____

(3) Identify the goal of your anger and proceed with gentleness.

Ask yourself "What am I hoping this episode produces?" You may have to admit that in your anger, you want to defeat and punish the other person. A quick and honest appraisal may force you to realize that you want the other person to feel guilty and worthless after you've finished. Silently admit your honest, ugly goal. Then refute it and replace it with the goal of solving the problem and respecting the person. With the right goal in mind, you can more rationally and constructively express your anger.

4. Be honest with yourself. What is frequently your subtle goal when you're angry?
   ❏ Gaining victory
   ❏ Administering punishment
   ❏ Producing humiliation
   ❏ Creating guilt
   ❏ Ridiculing
   ❏ Proving the other person wrong
   ❏ Other: _____

(4) Remember, conflict resolution always begins with questions rather than accusations.

How you present your anger largely determines how the other person receives it and responds to it. 1 Peter 3:9 encourages us not to return an insult for insult, but to give a blessing instead.

5. Since good conflict resolution always begins with questions, what questions might you need to ask someone you're angry with right now?

CONNECTING - 15 Minutes

LEADER INSTRUCTIONS FOR GROUP EXPERIENCE: Distribute full-size sheets of blank paper, and pens or pencils to each group member. Instruct people to write down all of the things that their former spouse has done and is doing that makes them angry. Tell them to be candid, because they won't have to share anything on this paper.

Next, have them write down ways they might be frustrated or angry with God. Assure them that they won't be struck by lightning. God already knows their anger and can handle it. To get them thinking, use these examples:
  - *If You hate divorce then why didn't You save my marriage?*
  - *Why are You letting my child(ren) suffer like this?*
  - *Why am I suffering when he/she is the one that wrecked our marriage?*
  - *You know the truth. Why did You let the judge approve that settlement or custody arrangement?*
Encourage them to write down their frustrations with God, their questions, and their accusations. Assure them that they won't have to share these either.

When everyone is finished, have the group wad their papers up into a tight ball. Have them really squeeze it hard and notice the tension in their forearms and hands. Pass the trash can around. Have each member unfold his or her paper ball, rip it into shreds, and throw it into the trash can.

1. Let's discuss our exercise. By wadding up your paper and throwing it into the trash, have you gotten rid of our anger? Why or Why not?

The truth is that the issues that made us angry are still with us even though we tore up our papers and threw them away. Your healing journey is a process. Even if you've somehow been able to eliminate all your anger to date, another encounter or issue will soon require you to reevaluate your anger management. Ongoing communication, negotiation, decision-making, and conflict resolution with your ex-spouse are realities and necessities, especially when children are involved. The good news is that anger does not have to consume or control you. You can learn to appropriately respond to anger, and choose to constructively express your anger in healthy ways.

2. What do you find most difficult about communicating with God? What do you think it is that causes you to struggle in this area?

3. What do you find most difficult about communicating with your ex-spouse? What inside of you makes this difficult for you?

God is with us. We're all in this together. From this point on, we'll work side by side to manage our anger in healthy and godly ways. What are specific ways that we can pray for you and support you this week?

My Prayer Requests:

My Group's Prayer Requests:

In addition to specific prayer requests, thank God for the journey you are on together and pray for the courage to identify and confront the roots of your anger.

TAKING IT HOME

LOOKING INWARD ... A QUESTION TO TAKE TO MY HEART:

Look into your heart for the answer to these questions. This is introspection time—time to grapple with what drives your thinking and behavior. <u>Every action has a corresponding belief that drives it.</u> Dig for what you believe in the deep recesses of your heart about God, yourself, and the world in which you live. Be sure to capture your thoughts.

❋ How do I express my anger in ungodly or unhealthy ways? What's really behind this? What messages do I hear playing over and over in my mind about God, myself, or my ex-spouse that are driving my angry reaction?

LOOKING UPWARD ... A QUESTION TO TAKE TO GOD:

When you ask God a question, expect His Spirit to respond to your heart. Be careful not to rush it, or manufacture an answer. Don't jot down your idea of the "right answer." Don't turn the Bible into a reference book or spiritual encyclopedia. Just pose the question to God, and wait on Him to speak personally in a fresh way. The litmus test for anything we hear from God is alignment with the Bible as our ultimate truth source. Always write down what you hear from God.

❋ God, it's not easy to admit that I'm angry at You. What do You think of my anger toward You? What would You like to tell me about my anger toward You? How do You feel about my divorce?

Looking Forward ... Prepare for Session 4

Please capture your thoughts and feelings in the "My Forgiveness Journal" on the next page, as you continue on your healing journey. Consider these questions that will be discussed in Session 4:

1. What is my first and candid response to being told that I needed to forgive my ex-spouse?

2. Complete this sentence: I find it difficult or impossible to forgive my ex-spouse because ...

3. Do I view the connection between forgiveness and reconciliation of a relationship?

4. What do I imagine my ex-spouse's response would be if I explained that I had forgiven him or her?

MY FORGIVENESS JOURNAL

EXPERIENCING THE FREEDOM OF FORGIVENESS

BREAKING THE ICE – 15 MINUTES

LEADER: Many of the people in your group may have experienced a tough week of wrestling with God or their hearts. The "Breaking the Ice" questions will help start the session on a lighter note, and continue to help the group connect a little more. Try to keep the tone upbeat and fun. To be sure everyone gets a turn, but encourage people to be brief.

1. Complete this sentence: When I was a child or teenager, the most embarrassing thing anyone ever did to me was …

2. Help your group get to know you better. Using the following word-pairs, select words that best describe you. Take turns sharing your highlights.

Impulsive	Cautious
Relaxed	Tense
Self-confident	Unsure
Modest	Boastful
Mature	Childish
Childlike	Stuffy
Agreeable	Disagreeable
Spontaneous	Predictable
Close	Distant
Friendly	Aloof
Compassionate	Flexible
Industrious	Lazy
Straightforward	Indirect
Ambitious	Complacent
Competitive	Noncompetitive
Generous	Stingy
Happy	Sad

3. How did your "Taking It Home" assignments go? How about the question you asked of God this week? Did God tell you how He felt about your divorce?

4. If a judge gave my ex-spouse jail time for how much he or she has hurt me (and my family), I think he or she would be sentenced to:
   ❒ Probation and community service
   ❒ 1 week in jail and $5,000 fine
   ❒ 1 year in county jail with laundry duty and no TV privileges
   ❒ 2 years in jail with one month of solitary confinement
   ❒ 5-10 years in the state penitentiary
   ❒ Life sentence with no chance of parole
   ❒ Other: _____

5. Complete this sentence: I find it difficult or impossible to forgive my ex-spouse because ...

OPENING PRAYER
God, forgiveness seems impossible and unreasonable to us. Resentment has become our roommate, but You say it must be evicted. We know our anger needs some place to go. Jesus, our Forgiver, help us have the courage to forgive.

Last week we explored the emotion of anger, and learned that it's a natural response to the maddening circumstances surrounding divorce. Hopefully this past week we've approached a familiar emotion with some new thoughts and behaviors. This week we want to confront the issue of anger, and carry it into radical, unfamiliar territory—the realm of forgiveness.

OBJECTIVES FOR THIS SESSION:
- Increase our openness to the radical concept of forgiveness
- Recognize what true forgiveness is and is not
- Understand the benefits of forgiveness and consequences of unforgiveness
- Confront our resistance to forgiveness
- With God's help, begin the process of forgiveness

DISCOVERING THE TRUTH – 35 MINUTES

LEADER: *In the initial part of "Discovering the Truth," you will begin to share with the group what forgiveness is not. Invite various members of your group to read the explanations. Be sure to leave time for the "Embracing the Truth and "Connecting" segments later in this session.*

1. How would you explain what forgiveness is?

God referring to His people says ...
I will forgive their wickedness and will remember their sins no more.   JEREMIAH 31:34B (NIV)

2. How does God forgive according to Jeremiah?

FORGIVENESS ISN'T ...

Before we define what genuine forgiveness is and make a case for its necessity in healing, let's first clarify what forgiveness is not.

(1) Forgiveness is NOT forgetting

We frequently hear the phrase "forgive and forget," but forgiveness does not imply some form of amnesia. When the Bible says that God "will remember their sins no more" it doesn't mean that He suddenly has no recall of an offense. It means that God does not catalog our sin and use the information against us.

(2) Forgiveness is NOT minimizing the hurt

Forgiveness does not water down the offense by saying something like, "It's OK, it wasn't that bad," or "I know you didn't mean to hurt me." The truth is you've been hurt deeply and, perhaps, quite intentionally. Forgiveness does not say, "I'm alright; it's just a flesh wound." It does not give a parking ticket for vehicular manslaughter. Instead, forgiveness calls the violation what it is just like an umpire calls what he sees.

(3) Forgiveness is NOT necessarily reconciliation

Perhaps you were thinking, " If I forgive my ex-spouse, I have to initiate or at least be receptive to reconciliation." Truthfully, some of you are already open to reconciliation, and would give anything for it to happen, but reconciliation isn't even on the radar screen of your former spouse. Others have left the wreckage of a marriage where you've been mistreated for years even before the divorce. The thought of a required reconciliation feels like being sentenced to life in prison without parole. Forgiveness recognizes that reconciliation is usually either not possible or not wise following a divorce.

3. Which of these three qualifiers about what forgiveness isn't has you breathing a sigh of relief? Do any of these alter the view you've carried about forgiveness?

4. Do these qualifiers make you more open to being a forgiving ex-spouse? Explain.

LEADER: *Have a group member read Colossians 3:12-13 aloud. At times there are related personal application questions. However, most of the application questions appear in the "Embracing the truth" section.*

FORGIVENESS IS TOUGH

[12] Therefore, as God's chosen people, holy and dearly loved, clothe yourselves with heartfelt compassion, kindness, humility, gentleness and patience. [13] Bear with each other and forgive whatever grievances you may have against another. Forgive just as the Lord forgave you.

COLOSSIANS 3:12-13 (NIV)

Read the first part of that verse again and insert your ex-spouse's name: "... clothe myself with heartfelt kindness, humility, gentleness and patience toward _____. "

5. What's your honest reaction to this command from Scripture when you realize that it also applies to forgiving your ex-spouse?

Doesn't something inside of you revolt at forgiving someone who has hurt you so deeply? Show kindness, gentleness, and patience toward him or her? You've got to be kidding! Do you know what he or she has done to me? The scum bag don't deserve forgiveness!

Being a Christ-follower is quite a challenge. In Matthew 5, Jesus says, "Bless those who curse you," and "If you only show kindness to those who show kindness to you, big deal! Tax collectors and total pagans are nice to each other, so what makes you different?"

6. What is significant about the instruction in Colossians 3:13 to "forgive just as the Lord forgave you"?

LEADER: *The questions that follow will help people understand that Jesus calls us to extend the same forgiveness we have received. Have a volunteer read the following parable aloud to the group.*

A HEART OF FORGIVENESS

Jesus told the story of a slave who owed a king a huge sum of money (10,000 talents), and yet was forgiven his entire debt by the king. Let's see how he responded to this immense mercy ...

[28] *But that slave went out and found one of his fellow slaves who owed him 100 denarii. He grabbed him, started choking him, and said, "Pay what you owe!"*
[29] *At this, his fellow slave fell down and began begging him, "Be patient with me, and I will pay you back."* [30] *But he wasn't willing. On the contrary, he went and threw him into prison until he could pay what was owed.* [31] *When the other slaves saw what had taken place, they were deeply distressed and went and reported to their master everything that had happened.* [32] *Then, after he had summoned him, his master said to him, "You wicked slave! I forgave you all that debt because you begged me.* [33] *Shouldn't you also have had mercy on your fellow slave, as I had mercy on you?"* [34] *And his master got angry and handed him over to the jailers until he could pay everything that was owed.* [35] *So My heavenly Father will also do to you if each of you does not forgive his brother from his heart.*
MATTHEW 18:21-35 (HCSB)

7. What obstacle that prevents us from extending forgiveness does Jesus highlight in this story of the unforgiving slave (Matthew 18:28-35)?

[44] Then turning to the woman, but speaking to Simon, he [Jesus] said, "Do you see this woman? I came to your home: you provided no water for my feet, but she rained tears on my feet and dried them with her hair. [45] You gave me no greeting, but from the time I arrived she hasn't quit kissing my feet. [46] You provided nothing for freshening up, , but she has soother my feet with perfume. Impressive, isn't it? [47] She was forgiven many, many sins, and so she is very, very grateful. If the forgiveness is minimal, the gratitude is minimal."

LUKE 7:44-46 (THE MESSAGE)

8. What is the point of Luke 7 on this issue of forgiveness?

9. Be honest with yourself. What do you think your ex-spouse "owes" you? How could he or she pay enough to really satisfy you?

Jesus' act of forgiveness on the cross helps us to understand what forgiveness really is. The original meaning of "forgive" suggests the canceling of a debt.

- Bitterness says, "You owe me, big time!"

- Resentment declares, "I'll make sure you pay for this for the rest of your life!"

- Forgiveness says, "I'm canceling your debt. You don't owe me any emotional compensation or restitution." On the cross when Jesus said, "It is finished," He used "*tetelestai,*" an accounting term meaning "paid in full." He fully paid our sin debt by dying on the cross.

Jesus points out that one obstacle that prevents us from extending forgiveness to others is that we don't fully recognize our own need for forgiveness from God. We really don't think our sin is all that bad, so God's forgiveness is really not much of a stretch for Him. Grace is not really that amazing until you realize your own desperate need for it.

Do you see the connection? Our awareness of our own need for forgiveness increases our gratitude, worship, and love of Christ. It also compels us to extend forgiveness to others ... no matter how deeply they have hurt us.

EMBRACING THE TRUTH – 20 MINUTES

LEADER: *During this "Embracing the Truth" time, we'll discuss the path to forgiveness. Remind group members, that forgiveness will not happen overnight, but it's a process each one must be committed to if they are going to freed from the bondage of resentment and bitterness.*

BENEFITS AND CONSEQUENCES

We believe the lie that our anger is effectively punishing the offender. But, the truth is that it's we, in fact, who are imprisoned. Frederick Buechner writes in *Wishful Thinking,*

> *Of the Seven Deadly Sins, anger is possibly the most fun. To lick your wounds, to smack your lips over grievances long past, to roll over your tongue the prospect of bitter confrontations still to come, to savor to the last toothsome morsel both the pain you are given and the pain you are giving back—in many ways it is a feast fit for a king. The chief drawback is that what you are wolfing down is yourself. The skeleton at the feast is you.*

When we choose to forgive, we release our prisoner from the dungeon and discover that we are subsequently freed from the dank cell of our own bitterness. Spiritually and emotionally, forgiveness frees us.

1. On a scale of 1 to 10, what would it mean to you to walk in the freedom of forgiveness?

1.............2.............3.............4.............5.............6.............7.............8.............9.............10
I don't care!   I'm considering it   It's tough, but I want it   I'd pay any price

2. How has withholding forgiveness held you captive spiritually and emotionally?

3. What are the benefits of forgiving the villain in your story? Is there anyone else in the story that you need to forgive who stands to benefit from your forgiveness? Explain.

We've clarified what forgiveness is not, but how will we know when we have actually forgiven our ex-spouse? Clyde Besson, a tenured worker in the field of divorce recovery, suggests that <u>you know you have progressed toward genuine forgiveness when you discover within yourself the capacity to wish for good things to happen to the one who hurt you instead of calamity and disaster.</u>

That's a very specific and reasonable indicator of forgiveness. It does not imply absent-mindedness of the hurt, minimizing or trivializing the offense, or presuming reconciliation. But remember, forgiveness is not an event, but a process of divine work by the Holy Spirit in you. Forgiveness does not come naturally to us, even if we become convinced of its necessity and benefits. To forgive we must swim upstream against a raging downstream current of hurt and anger. Lewis Smedes writes, "When we forgive someone who has wounded us, we dance to the rhythm of a divine heartbeat."

4. What are two Scriptures, statements, principles, or ideas from today's lesson that you realize you need to apply to your life?

5. What is your next baby step toward walking in the freedom of forgiveness?

CONNECTING – 20 MINUTES

LEADER: Use this "Connecting" time to develop more closeness within your group, as well as to encourage and support one another in practical ways throughout the week. Invite everyone to join in and be open and supportive with each other.

LEADER INSTRUCTIONS FOR GROUP EXPERIENCE: Prior to the session, set up the TV/DVD player with the movie *Les Misérables*, starring Liam Neeson. Watch Scenes 2-4 (past the credits from 02:55 to 09:52 minutes on the DVD) through the dramatic close-up conversation between the priest and Jean Valjean after the priest gives Valjean the silver candlesticks. Then, have the group answer the questions below.

As we watch the opening scene from a classic story, *Les Miserables*, be aware of the messages of forgiveness.

1. In this film, what strikes you about the priest's capacity to forgive Jean, who both stole from him, and physically hurt him?

2. Put yourself in Jean Valjean's place. What does it feel like to be forgiven and shown grace instead of the punishment you deserve?

3. What are specific ways that we can pray for you and support you this week in your journey of forgiveness?

My Prayer Requests:

My Group's Prayer Requests:

In addition to specific prayer requests, thank God for His forgiveness. Pray for a divine capacity to forgive and free your ex-spouses ... and yourselves. Ask God to supernaturally remove any resistance to forgiving.

Taking It Home

Looking Inward ... A Question to Take to My Heart:

Look into your heart for the answer to these questions. This is introspection time—time to grapple with what drives your thinking and behavior. <u>Every action has a corresponding belief that drives it.</u> Dig for what you believe in the deep recesses of your heart about God, yourself, and the world in which you live. Be sure to capture your thoughts.

⁕ What does my answer to the "Jail Time" icebreaker question early in this session reveal about my level of bitterness toward my ex-spouse?

⁕ What does my attitude toward my ex-spouse reveal about my beliefs regarding God's concern for me?

Looking Upward ... A Question to Take to God:

When you ask God a question, expect His Spirit to respond to your heart. Be careful not to rush it, or manufacture an answer. Don't jot down your idea of the "right answer." Don't turn the Bible into a reference book or spiritual encyclopedia. Just pose the question to God, and wait on Him to speak personally in a fresh way. The litmus test for anything we hear from God is alignment with the Bible as our ultimate truth source. Always write down what you hear from God.

⁕ God, how have I sinned against You and others, even my ex-spouse? What do I need to ask forgiveness for? What do You want to show me about forgiving?

Looking Forward ... Prepare for Session 5

Please capture your thoughts and feelings in the "My Concerns Journal" below, as you work through your healing process. Consider these questions that will be discussed in Session 5:

1. What do I worry about the most since my divorce?

2. What issue that is not connected to my divorce currently causes me great concern? (For example: parent's health, teenager's behavior, job security, other relationships, or personal inadequacy for the challenges.)

3. Complete the following sentence: "When I think about the future..."
   ❒ I am very optimistic. I imagine the best.
   ❒ I am somewhat optimistic. I imagine good things happening.
   ❒ I am somewhat pessimistic. I foresee several problems.
   ❒ I am both optimistic and pessimistic. I like to call it being realistic.
   ❒ I am very pessimistic. I tend to imagine the worst.
   ❒ Other: _____

My Concerns Journal

RISING FROM THE PARALYSIS OF WORRY

BREAKING THE ICE - 15 MINUTES

> *LEADER: The first "Breaking the Ice" question should be fun as you start the session. You'll learn more about each other's stories as you dive into the other questions. The goal as always is to give everyone a chance to participate in responding to questions.*

1. Which of the following statements would likely cause you the greatest anxiety?
   - ❏ Your dentist saying, "You need a root canal."
   - ❏ Your son saying, "Before you see the car, let me explain."
   - ❏ The tech guy at the office saying, "You lost everything on the hard drive."
   - ❏ Your mother saying, "He (she) seemed so nice; I just had to give him (her) your phone number."
   - ❏ Your daughter saying, "I'm going to Ft. Lauderdale for spring break."
   - ❏ Your son saying, "I think I'd like to be a hairdresser."
   - ❏ Your boss saying, "Come on in and close the door."
   - ❏ Other: _____

2. My approach to worry is to:
   - ❏ Lay awake at night and imagine the worst
   - ❏ Avoid the worry by becoming busy or immersing myself in entertainment
   - ❏ Smother the worry with chocolate or other "comfort food"
   - ❏ Force myself to think rationally about the issue
   - ❏ Pray, pray, pray
   - ❏ Talk it out, and get feedback
   - ❏ Other: _____

3. Evaluate the approach you checked above. How is it working for you so far? Explain.

4. Would you share a key insight about forgiveness that you gained from the question that you took to your heart or the question you asked of God this week? Others in the group will benefit from your insights and responses.

5. Complete the following sentence, which you considered in your homework: "When I think about the future ..."
   ❐ I am very optimistic. I imagine the best.
   ❐ I am somewhat optimistic. I imagine good things happening.
   ❐ I am somewhat pessimistic. I foresee several problems.
   ❐ I am both optimistic and pessimistic. I like to call it being realistic.
   ❐ I am very pessimistic. I tend to imagine the worst.
   ❐ Other: _____

OPENING PRAYER

Lord, we don't have to try to worry. It comes naturally to us. It's like the revved engine on a Formula One racecar. Something stressful happens that presses our buttons, and our thoughts and feelings torque our anxiety factor into high gear. Father, we desire a different way to think and live that isn't paralyzed by worry. Please speak into our hearts today.

WORRY SABOTAGES US

Over the past weeks we have dealt with the issues of loss, depression, anger, and forgiveness. Now we come to the foot of the mountain called Worry. It seems like an insurmountable peak, and our backpacks are heavy with hurts and fears. Overcome Mount Worry? You expect me to climb that? Our alternative is to sit down and quit. We can justify giving in by telling ourselves that worry is our only reasonable response given the dire straights we're in. However, once we realize that worry wants to sabotage our health and growth, we will discover the strength to continue the climb.

Much of what causes us to worry is launched from conversations we have with others. Ultimately, however, it is our silent, internal conversations that script our worrisome anxiety. How do you change your internal script and edit your worries? That is the focus of today's session.

OBJECTIVES FOR THIS SESSION:
- Identify our surface and root worries, and acknowledge them to God
- Understand the role of prayer in the midst of our anxiety
- Prepare to move forward together on the healing journey

DISCOVERING THE TRUTH – 35 MINUTES

LEADER: *In the initial part of "Discovering the Truth" you will examine what Paul has to say about the topic of worry. To keep group members involved, invite various members of your group to read the Bible passages and questions aloud. After this topic, you'll study prayer's impact on worry. Be sure to leave time for the "Embracing the Truth" and "Connecting" segments of your session.*

THE INCARCERATED COUNSELOR

Paul's therapeutic counsel for anxiety is credible because he personally modeled the treatment plan and demonstrated its success. Remember that Paul is in prison facing possible execution when he wrote these words. When a man who is inching his way along death row says, "You don't have to be a prisoner of worry," you want to hear him out. In today's lesson, we'll study the words of Paul, our incarcerated counselor.

⁴ Rejoice in the Lord always; again I will say, rejoice! ⁵ Let your gentle spirit be known to all men. The Lord is near. ⁶ Be anxious (merimnaō) *for nothing, but in everything by prayer and supplication with thanksgiving let your requests be made known to God. ⁷ And the peace of God, which surpasses all comprehension, will guard your hearts and your minds in Christ Jesus. ... ¹⁰ But I rejoiced in the Lord greatly, that now at last you have revived your concern* (phroneō) *for me; indeed, you were concerned before, but you lacked opportunity.*

PHILIPPIANS 4:4-7,10 (NASB)

1. What's your gut level reaction to Paul's words, "Be anxious for nothing ..." or don't worry about anything? Do you think Paul really understands the kind the pressures of life dumps on us?

2. The Greek word for "anxious" (*merimnaō*) means "to worry or have a distracting care," and the word for "concern" (*phroneō*) means "to oversee or care for affectionately." So, what's the difference between good, healthy concern in verse 10 and unhealthy anxiety in verse 7?

LEADER: Use these questions to help group members interact about the concepts being discussed. Encourage open and honest dialogue and be sure to focus on accepting people where they are and encouraging them to take another step with God in the journey.

3. In your own words, describe the difference between anxiety and concern. Why do you think "anxiety" or "worry" is paralyzing and destructive, and "concern" is not?

4. Describe a time when you have personally been paralyzed by worry in your own experience.

5. What is Paul's prescription of paralyzing worry in Philippians 4:6-7? What do you think the command in verse 6 means and does not mean? What is the result promised?

We see in these verses that it's okay to be concerned, but it's bad to be anxious. The verb tense for *merimnaō* in Philippians 4:6 suggests ongoing worry without interruption. Actually, the verse could be translated: "Don't just sit and keep worrying ..." In other words, don't obsess and become fixated in worry. Don't just give in to worry and ride it like a treadmill to nowhere! Paul understands human nature, and his own experiences tell him that life in a fallen world produces anxious moments. However, being absolutely immobilized by worry is counterproductive, demonstrates a lack of faith, and does not resemble Christ.

WHY PRAYER WORKS

[36] *Then Jesus came with them to a place called Gethsemane, and said to His disciples, "Sit here while I go over there and pray."* [37] *And He took with Him Peter and the two sons of Zebedee, and began to be grieved and distressed.* [38] *Then He said to them, "My soul is deeply grieved, to the point of death; remain here and keep watch with Me."*

39 And He went a little beyond them, and fell on His face and prayed, saying, "My Father, if it is possible, let this cup pass from Me; yet not as I will, but as You will." ... 42 He went away again a second time and prayed, saying, "My Father, if this cannot pass away unless I drink it, Your will be done." ... 44 And He left them again, and went away and prayed a third time, saying the same thing once more. 45 Then He came to the disciples and said to them, "... Behold, the hour is at hand and the Son of Man is being betrayed into the hands of sinners. 46 "Get up, let us be going; behold, the one who betrays Me is at hand!"

MATTHEW 26:36-46 (NASB)

6. What was Jesus' state of mind before prayer (verses 37-38)? How about after His time of wrestling in prayer (verses 45-46)?

7. When Jesus prayed, it worked. How do you think prayer can effectively replace worry with peace?

8. Which of the following best describes how you pray when you're worried?
   - ❏ Fast food – A quick request with the expectation that my order will come momentarily.
   - ❏ Lean Cuisine® – My motive is to be transformed into something beautiful.
   - ❏ Gourmet meal – A five course prayer session with evaluation to follow.
   - ❏ Leftover lasagna – A little stale but I need the nourishment.
   - ❏ All-You-Can-Eat Buffet – Long prayers about everything under the sun but when they're completed I still feel overwhelmed.
   - ❏ Other: _____

9. What is the dynamic going on inside you when it's so hard to go to God during anxious or worry-filled times?

The power of prayer is not some hocus-pocus magic formula of saying the right words. There's two key reasons that prayer works:

(1) God's Presence

When you're in prayer, you're in the presence of Jehovah - Shalom, the Lord our Peace. There is peace in His presence. The command "fear not ..." is repeated 365 times (one for each day of the year!) in Scripture, and it is most often followed by "... for I am with you." God wants us to understand that His presence always brings peace. All we need to do is open the door of our heart and invite Him in.

(2) God's Perspective:

When you're in prayer, you regain perspective and truth. Cathartic prayer (pour your heart out and you'll feel better prayer) doesn't work because prayer isn't just about talking; it's also about listening. Jesus went into the Garden of Gethsemane deeply distressed and troubled. We don't know what the Father said, but it's clear that it renewed Jesus' perspective by speaking truth into His life and peace into His heart.

Paul's prescription for worry is personal prayer. Certainly we are encouraged to enlist others to pray for us, but the verse implies that the "peace that surpasses all understanding" is a result of personal prayer by the one in need. This remarkable peace is not the prayer request, it is the prayer result.

EMBRACING THE TRUTH – 20 MINUTES

The realistic goal is not to eliminate worry from your life, but to tame it by not allowing it to run wild throughout your mind. Jesus has a moment of absolute torment in the Garden, and Paul undoubtedly spends many sleepless nights in prison thinking about his infant churches. A certain degree of worry is normal. In fact, a certain amount of worry is probably necessary to stir us from apathy to action. Worry, however, must be restrained.

A basketball coach once remarked before a playoff game against the Chicago Bulls, "We know we cannot shut Michael Jordan down, but if we can limit him to 30 points, we've got a real shot at winning." Likewise, we shall never totally eradicate worry's presence in our lives, but by following the Scripture's game plan, we can certainly limit its influence. Talking these steps will prevent worry from paralyzing your life.

STEP 1: Identify your "surface worry" and your "root worry," and then acknowledge those worries to God.

Most of our worries threaten one or both of our two vital needs: significance and security. Significance is about feeling important, valued, and approved, and security seeks to avoid danger, loneliness, and poverty.

When you start to feel anxious, first identify your surface worry. For example, I'm worried my position or even my entire department may be eliminated. Then, identify the root worry: I'm worried I won't be able to pay my bills and I may lose the house. The root worry perceives that your security is threatened. After you identify both the surface and root worry, acknowledge these to God.

STEP 2: Hear and rehearse God's truthful reassurance.

As we stated earlier in the session, Jesus' transformation in the Garden of Gethsemane was influenced more by what He heard from the Father than by what He said to Him. In John 8:32, Jesus says, "You will know the truth and the truth will set you free." Hearing and rehearsing God's reassuring truth has the power to set you free from the prison of debilitating worry. Allow God speak to you from His Word, the Bible, about where your significance and security lies. Get a copy of the *God's Promises* book that lists some of God's promises from Scripture.

LEADER: *If possible, have a copy of* God's Promises *to pass around. Class members' interest will be greater if they can see an example of the book.*

STEP 3: Act within the circle of your influence, and leave the rest to God.

As the saying goes, "Worrying does not empty tomorrow of its troubles; it only empties today of its strength." Jesus made the same assertion long ago when He said, "Who of you by worrying can add a single hour to his life?" Worry is useless unless it propels us to action. Our first action should be prayer, followed by a thoughtful action within our "circle of influence." This is just another way of saying, "Do what you can, and leave the rest to God." Worry often immobilizes us. Instead, it should cause us to respond with prayer, action, and more prayer.

1. What is a surface worry and a root worry that you've been dealing with lately?

2. Has God spoken any truth to you in the midst of your worry? If so, explain. If not, why do you think that might be?

3. Describe a specific area of your life in which you need to do what you can, and truly leave the rest to God to handle.

4. What's the most beneficial insight about prayer that you gained in today's session?
   ❏ I need to stop giving in to worry and focus on praying instead.
   ❏ I need to listen and hear God speak to me during prayer.
   ❏ In the Garden, what Jesus heard was likely more important than what He prayed.
   ❏ I must pray personally for myself in order to diffuse my worry.
   ❏ Peace is the by-product of genuine prayer.
   ❏ Other: _____

CONNECTING - 20 MINUTES

LEADER: Use this "Connecting" time to deepen the sense of community in your group.
PASS OUT 3 x 5" INDEX CARDS for QUESTION 1. Then, using the Group Experience, illustrate that it's only normal to feel a sense of apprehension or holding back when under pressure.

1. Spend a minute or two scanning back through today's session. What was the most meaningful Scripture, principle, idea, or statement in this session for you personally? Write the meaningful thought on a 3 x 5" index card; keep it in visible spot at home.

LEADER INSTRUCTIONS FOR GROUP EXPERIENCE: Be sensitive to each person's comfort level as you lead this experience. Have the group members gather around a seated member of the group and place their hands on the seated member's head, shoulders, and arms. Then, have the seated member try to stand up as the other group members attempt to prevent that from happening. Have the group offer resistance past the point of it being funny. The seated member should feel some frustration. Finally, have a group member extend a hand and help the seated member up. This process should be repeated so that every group member experiences the resistance followed the assistance to stand. When everyone has had a turn, answer the following questions as a group:

2. What was that like to attempt to stand, but have your best efforts and strength thwarted? How does this relate to the gravity of the worry?

3. What did you feel when someone finally helped you to stand?

4. What can this group do this week in a practical way to help you come to terms with the worry in your life? How can we pray for you today?

MY PRAYER REQUESTS:

MY GROUP'S PRAYER REQUESTS:

In addition to specific prayer requests, pray together for each person individually, that he or she will begin to see God's love and care and feel God's embrace and presence.

NOTE: Make a note to bring your favorite coffee mug or beverage container to the next meeting (Session 6).

Taking It Home

Looking Inward ... A Question to Take to My Heart:

Look into your heart for the answer to these questions. This is introspection time—time to grapple with what drives your thinking and behavior. <u>Every action has a corresponding belief that drives it.</u> Dig for what you believe in the deep recesses of your heart about God, yourself, and the world in which you live. Be sure to capture your thoughts.

* What am I currently the most worried about? What does this worry reveal about what I really believe about God or myself? (It's our behavior that best displays our truest beliefs, not what we think or say we believe.)

Looking Upward ... A Question to Take to God

When you ask God a question, expect His Spirit to respond to your heart. Be careful not to rush it, or manufacture an answer. Don't jot down your idea of the "right answer." Don't turn the Bible into a reference book or spiritual encyclopedia. Just pose the question to God, and wait on Him to speak personally in a fresh way. The litmus test for anything we hear from God is alignment with the Bible as our ultimate truth source. Always write down what you hear from God.

* Lord, I have a mixture of faith and doubt, trust and uncertainty. What do You want to say to me about this worry? Even if my worst case scenario were to happen, what would You want me to keep in mind?

Looking Forward ... Prepare for Session 6:

Please capture your thoughts and feelings in the "Season of Suffering Journal" on the next page, as you work through your healing process. Consider these questions that will be discussed in Session 6:

1. Before my divorce, what was most stressful or painful experience I ever had?

2. During that earlier traumatic season, did I respond to the suffering by moving closer to God or by moving away from Him? What reasoning or conclusions influenced this movement?

3. In this current season of pain caused by my divorce, do I find myself moving closer to God or moving away from Him? In what ways is this happening? What's driving this movement?

NOTE: Make a note to bring your favorite coffee mug or beverage container to the next meeting (Session 6).

Season of Suffering Journal

REDEEMING THE COST OF YOUR SUFFERING

BREAKING THE ICE – 15 MINUTES

> *LEADER: It's now week six of the study, and your group has shared a lot together. These "Breaking the Ice" questions will help you to continue to get to know each other, and launch the topic for today. Encourage everyone to participate in responding to the questions, but keep things moving.*

1. Unlock your memory box and share a little bit of your personal history. Choose one of the "firsts" listed below and take turns sharing your answers.
   - ❐ The first time I kissed someone ...
   - ❐ The first time I attended a formal event ...
   - ❐ The first time I tried to swim or jump off a diving board ...
   - ❐ The first time I did something adventurous or crazy ...
   - ❐ The first time I drove a car ...
   - ❐ The first time I got a traffic ticket ...

2. Describe for the group one of the worst physical injuries you experienced as a child, teen, or young adult.

3. Did you hear from God this week about your worry or anxiety? Did you gain new insights into what drives your worry? Please share what you learned. Others in the group will benefit from your insights and responses.

4. As you mentally prepared for this session on suffering, what surfaced about your past coping skills in dealing with stressful or painful events? In this season of pain caused by your divorce, do you find yourself moving closer to God or moving away from Him?

OPENING PRAYER

Lord, because of our divorce experiences, we sometimes feel homeless, like our emotional shelters have been destroyed. Help us to rebuild and find our homes in You. Draw us to the shelter beneath Your wings. Teach us to draw our strength from Your presence, Your truth, and Your love.

WOUNDED BY DIVORCE

In the previous session, we explored the common experience of worry. This week we'll seek to understand the suffering of divorce. Divorce is certainly one of the most painful and stressful of all human experiences. It causes both adults and children to suffer. In the midst of the suffering, we often ask hard questions like ... "If God hates divorce, why didn't He prevent mine?" and "How do I reconcile my experience of suffering with the belief that God is loving, good, all-knowing, and powerful?" In today's session, we hope to offer biblically sound answers to these questions as we move forward in our healing journeys.

We have all been wounded by divorce We all have scars from the battlefront. Our suffering has been intense, and we know that it isn't over yet. During this session, we'll learn to see our suffering from a different perspective as we realize there's hope embedded into our stories.

OBJECTIVES FOR THIS SESSION:
- Discover our drive to solve the mystery of suffering
- Recognize the hope Christians have in the midst of suffering
- Realize that God's goodness is very compatible with the existence of suffering
- Confront our unrealistic expectations concerning suffering
- Adopt some positive responses to suffering

DISCOVERING THE TRUTH – 30 MINUTES

LEADER: In the initial part of "Discovering the Truth," you will investigate what Paul has to say about suffering. Ask for volunteers to read the Bible passages. After this, you'll examine some unrealistic expectations we frequently have of God. There is a lot of content in this session ... Keep things moving at a steady pace through "Discovering the Truth" and "Embracing the Truth." Leave ample time for the "Connecting" time.

FAULTY CONCLUSIONS

Trouble comes in shapes, sizes, and colors as varied as a child's box of Legos®.
When confronted with crisis and suffering, we are tempted to conclude one of the following about God:

- God is indifferent and aloof.
- God is not powerful or engaged enough to prevent or resolve my pain.
- God is focused on more important matters than my pain.

When we agree with one of these faulty conclusions, we pull away from God. Media giant and avowed atheist, Ted Turner, told a reporter that as a result of observing his sister's suffering and death, he concluded that there was no God. Pop icon Madonna acknowledged that as a child, the death of her mother was a turning point that led her to reject much of the teaching she'd received about God. Suffering is indeed life-changing.

1. Which of the following responses have you had in the midst of suffering? Check all that apply.
   - ❏ God does not exist.
   - ❏ God does not care.
   - ❏ God isn't powerful enough.
   - ❏ God must be testing me.
   - ❏ God must be punishing me for something.
   - ❏ God must be trying to teach me a lesson.
   - ❏ God is absent.
   - ❏ God is silent.
   - ❏ Other: _____

LEADER: Share with your class about a season of suffering that you have experienced, either past or current. What is one of the toughest things you've gone through? Were you tempted to draw a faulty conclusion like those listed above?

PRESSED ON EVERY SIDE, BUT NOT CRUSHED

The Apostle Paul experienced a life of hardships, persecution, imprisonment, beatings, and even attempts to kill him because of his commitment to live in the larger story and share Jesus throughout the Roman Empire.

⁷ But this precious treasure—this light and power that now shine in us—is held in a perishable container, that is, in our weak bodies. Everyone can see that the glorious power within must be from God and is not our own. ⁸ We are pressed on every side, but not crushed and broken. We are perplexed because we don't know why things happen as they do, but we don't give up and quit. ⁹ We are hunted down, but God never abandons us. We are knocked down, but we get up again and keep going.

2 CORINTHIANS 4:7-9 (THE LIVING BIBLE)

This passage can be diagrammed as four couplets to communicate Paul's message.

We will likely experience this:	But we have this hope:
(1) Pressed on every side ...	but we're not crushed and broken.
(2) Perplexed and don't know why ...	but we don't give up and quit.
(3) We are hunted down (persecuted) ...	but we're never abandoned.
(4) We are knocked down ...	but we can get up and keep going.

2. In what ways can you relate to Paul's struggles in 2 Corinthians 4? What pressures do you feel right now that you'd be willing to share with the group?

3. What core truths do you think Paul embraced that enabled him to experience intense pressure, confusion, persecution, and abuse without giving in to despair? What kept him going?

You may be thinking, "But I *am* being crushed from the pressure!" Take heart! There's a difference between *feeling* crushed and actually *being* crushed. Paul tells us that even devoted Christ-followers will often feel squeezed by life issues and circumstances. But Jesus gives hope when life threatens to steal our joy, suffocate our hope, and crush our spirit.

The Mystery of Suffering

Many godly men in the Bible questioned God in the midst of their suffering. The Midianites have been terrorizing God's people for years, when the angel of the Lord showed up.

[12] Then the Angel of the LORD appeared to him and said: "The LORD is with you, mighty warrior." [13] Gideon said to Him, "Please Sir, if the LORD is with us, why has all this happened? And where are all His wonders that our fathers told us about? They said, 'Hasn't the LORD brought us out of Egypt?' But now the LORD has abandoned us and handed us over to Midian."

JUDGES 6:12-13 (HCSB)

Strong spiritual leaders of Israel penned the psalms, and many people for centuries have sung the praises to God in the Psalms, but we seldom sing the emotional hurts.

[9] I will say to God, my rock, "Why have You forgotten me? Why must I go about in sorrow because of the enemy's oppression?" [10] My adversaries taunt me, as if crushing my bones, while all day long they say to me, "Where is your God?" [11] Why am I so depressed? Why this turmoil within me?

PSALM 42:9-11A (HCSB)

4. What is the heart of Gideon's and the Psalmist's questions? Rephrase what they ask in today's language.

5. What do you think the basic presupposition was behind both questions?

"Why?" is a natural question because we, as humans, are compelled to make sense of our world. We don't deal well with ambiguity. We want clarity and answers. It's the question people have asked from the beginning: "Why do bad things happen to good people?"

6. Have you felt pounded or knocked down by your divorce? If so, when? What happened?

7. As devastating as your divorce has been, share how you not have been destroyed by it. What evidence shows that you are able to get up and begin to move forward?

Unrealistic Expectations

Almost everyone has subtle beliefs and expectations about how life and God should work. Our core beliefs and expectations make sense to us, but they are often not grounded in Scripture. "His ways are not our ways" the Bible warns, and yet we are prone to interpret God and life from our own perspective and desires. Let's look at three subtle and problematic expectations we frequently have of God.

EXPECTATION 1: The Expectation of Immunity

Tommy Wier, a pastor and black belt in karate, describes a day in a class in which the lesson involved self-defense against someone attacking with a knife. When the instructor demonstrated to the students how to use their legs and forearms to take the non-lethal cuts before either escaping or defeating the attacker, Tommy interrupted the instructor by saying, "Excuse me, but I'd like to know how to avoid being cut at all!" The instructor replied, "Tommy, this isn't Hollywood. When someone is attacking you with a knife, you will be cut. Once you accept being cut, you can concentrate on not being killed."

8. Can you relate to Tommy in this story when you think about the struggles in your life? Please explain. How do you feel about what the instructor explained?

A joyful life is not void of pain and suffering. It's clear, as we've considered some godly people, that God's children are not immune to pain and suffering.

EXPECTATION 2: The Expectation of an Explanation

[11] *When I was a child, I spoke like a child, I thought like a child, I reasoned like a child. When I became a man, I put aside childish things.* [12] *For now we see indistinctly, as in a mirror, but then face to face. Now I know in part, but then I will know fully, as I am fully known.*

1 CORINTHIANS 13:11-12 (HCSB)

9. According to 1 Corinthians 13:12, what's our ability to make sense of it all? Why do you think God seldom answers our "Why?" question?

Author Philip Yancey writes, "Perhaps God keeps us ignorant because enlightenment might not help us. Perhaps God keeps us ignorant because we are incapable of comprehending the answer." Scripture says, "We see indistinctly." Our "Why?" question is not really an intellectual inquiry that can be satisfied with facts. Rather, it is an emotional question that seeks reassurance and comfort.

EXPECTATION 3: The Expectation of Rapid Relief

Friends of Daniel, Shadrach, Meshach, and Abdnego had refused to bow down to the golden statue of the king of Babylon and were sentenced to death in a fiery furnace.

[17] If we are thrown into the blazing furnace, the God we serve is able to save us from it, and he will rescue us from your hand, O king. [18] "But even if he does not, we want you to know, O king, that we will not serve your gods or worship the image of gold you have set up.

DANIEL 3:17-18 (NIV)

10. What did Shadrach, Meshach, and Abdnego understand about pain and suffering that we don't get in our modern culture? What is the problem with a relentless pursuit of answering the "Why?" question?

Many Christians have put God on "probation" because He's not doing His job of preventing suffering or at least bringing quick relief from it. Christian psychologist Larry Crabb makes this challenging assessment, "We treat personal discomfort as the central evil from which we need to be saved. When we blend the pursuit of comfort with Christianity, Jesus becomes a divine masseur whose demands we heed only after we are properly relaxed. But that is not the Christianity of the Bible. Christ offers hope, not relief, in the middle of suffering, and He commands us to pursue Him hotly even when we'd rather stop and look after our own well-being."

EMBRACING THE TRUTH – 20 MINUTES

1. Which of these three subtle expectations do you struggle with the most? Discuss this.
   - ❏ I expect immunity from suffering.
   - ❏ I demand to know why the suffering occurred.
   - ❏ I require that the suffering be promptly alleviated.

Let's look at some steps that can help us to adopt some positive responses to suffering:

STEP 1: Accept the reality of problems.

Dear friends, do not be surprised at the painful trial you are suffering, as though something StRaNGe were happening to you. But rejoice that you participate in the sufferings of Christ, <u>so that you may be overjoyed when His glory is revealed</u>.

1 PETER 4:12 (NIV)

2. What purpose do our present sufferings net for us? How do the struggles we're experiencing compare to what we have to gain?

We typically respond to a crisis in our lives like a diner who finds some strange foreign object floating in his or her soup. "What is this?! Waiter! Waiter!" When we expect God to prevent or relieve us of suffering, we only add to our stress. Faith does not demand a life with no wounds, but knows how to survive the wounds and live large in spite of them. As Larry Crabb phrases it, "Finding God in this life does not mean building a house in a land of no storms; rather, it means building a house that no storm can destroy."

3. What's your reaction to Crabb's quote?

STEP 2: Draw support from others.

Carry one another's burdens GALATIANS 6:2 (HCSB)

Let us consider how we may spur one another on to love and good deeds. HEBREWS 10:24 (NIV)

4. According to Galatians 6 and Hebrews 10, where is our support supposed to come from? Where specifically does your support come from when life doesn't make sense?

Even as we drop our expectation that life be crisis-free, God doesn't expect us to merely tough out our crises in private self-determination like spiritual Lone Rangers. He's given us Christian community. Larry Crabb says, "Soul care requires two kinds of relationships: spiritual friendship and spiritual direction. Both exist only as a part of Christian community."

Ideally, your spiritual community should come looking for you, but the search party may need help to find you. Send up a flare! Seek help from a friend, pastor, counselor, or supportive group like this one.

STEP 3: Offer support to others

He comforts us in all our affliction, so that we may be able to comfort those who are in any kind of affliction, through the comfort we ourselves receive from God.

2 CORINTHIANS 1:4 (HCSB)

5. What redemption formula has God put into place in 2 Corinthians 1:4.? Discuss the implications for you individually, and for this group?

Don't waste your suffering! Use it to help others and redeem your pain. Eddie and Gail lead a GriefShare support group in their church. Both Eddie and Gail have experienced tragic loss. Gail's first husband died in a car accident when their first child was just a toddler. Eddie's teenage daughter from his first marriage was murdered. In recent years, death has also claimed their aged parents. Eddie and Gail don't have counseling degrees, but they are uniquely qualified to minister to grieving people. Their grief ministry has not eliminated their sense of loss, but it's redeeming their pain. Their greatest brokenness has become the platform of their most significant ministry.

6. What core truth have you learned experientially that could help someone who is newly separated or divorced?

CONNECTING – 25 MINUTES

LEADER INSTRUCTIONS FOR GROUP EXPERIENCE: In preparation for this "Connecting" time, ask your group members beforehand to bring their favorite coffee mug or beverage container to this meeting. If you forgot to mention this at the end of last week's session, contact group members by phone or e-mail before this session and give them the simple assignment.

SHOW & TELL – During this "Connecting" time, ask the group members to display their mug or glass and answer these two questions:
(1) "Why is this your favorite mug or glass?" (2) "What does this mug or glass say about you?"

If people forget to bring a mug, simply ask them to describe their favorite beverage container, and answer the questions. NOTE: You will need to bring extra mugs or cups to provide them for the communion time that's coming up.

In the anxious moments before his arrest, Jesus prayed for God's will to be done, not His own. He drank from a cup of suffering which we are unfamiliar with, and He drank from the cup so that we would not have to. Before the group takes communion together, your leader will guide you in a "listening prayer time."

LISTENING PRAYER TIME:
You're going to lead group members in a short time of listening prayer.
- *Allow this experience some time; don't rush it.*
- *Put on quiet background music (use the CD* Pursued by God: Redemptive Worship Volume 1 *from Serendipity House, or select your own music); dim the lights if possible.*
- *Help each person create a small personal area. This is not a time to chat; make it very honoring.*
- *Trust God to speak to each person individually.*

DIRECTIONS ... *Ask your group members to close their eyes, and envision Jesus sitting right here in the room. Then, read Hebrews 4:15-16 from* The Message *paraphrase of the Bible: "We don't have a priest who is out of touch with our reality. He's been through weakness and testing, experienced it all—all but the sin. So let's walk right up to him and get what he is so ready to give. Take the mercy, accept the help." Pause, and then instruct group members to:*

1. Ask Jesus to show you how He feels about your struggles, your failures, and your pain.

2. Now ask Him how He feels about you.

3. Accept Jesus' mercy and help ... allow that burden of suffering and shame to lift off of you.

LEADER INSTRUCTIONS FOR GROUP EXPERIENCE: *In preparation for this time, gather beforehand a loaf or loaves of Italian or French bread, grape juice, and extra mugs or cups to give to group members that forgot to bring their own.*

COMMUNION EXPERIENCE:

NOTE: *If you or your church leadership are uncomfortable with you leading the communion or Eucharist experience, be sure to invite your pastor, minister, priest or church leader to serve communion. This experience will most likely be one of the most meaningful moments in this series.*

Distribute a torn loaf of Italian or French bread. Have each person tear off a small morsel and hold it. Read these lines aloud:
"The bread in our hands represents the body of the Lord Jesus, beaten and broken as a criminal even though He was without sin. He endured the humiliation and the pain because His commitment to be our acceptable sacrifice was greater than His craving for relief and rest. As we place the bread in our mouth, we taste the seasoning of His suffering, and we seek to ingest gratitude for grace. Take and eat."

Pour a small portion of grape juice into each group member's cup. Read these lines aloud:
"The juice in our cups represents the blood of the Lord Jesus that was shed for the forgiveness and removal of our sins. Jesus considered no cost too great to pay to reconcile us to Himself. We are humbled by such love. We embrace it and celebrate it, and we lift our cups in honor of His majesty. As we drink, we desire to drink in the wonder of His love and taste the flavor of His mercy. Drink deeply."

Allow group members time to sit quietly with God and celebrate His amazing love. After a couple of minutes, close this time in prayer. Ask for any personal prayer requests.

MY PRAYER REQUESTS:

MY GROUP'S PRAYER REQUESTS:

In addition to specific prayer requests, thank God for His love and sacrifice. Ask Him to redeem your brokenness, and use you to encourage and help others along the journey.

TAKING IT HOME

LOOKING INWARD ... A QUESTION TO TAKE TO MY HEART:

Look into your heart for the answer to these questions. This is introspection time—time to grapple with what drives your thinking and behavior. <u>Every action has a corresponding belief that drives it.</u> Dig for what you believe in the deep recesses of your heart about God, yourself, and the world in which you live. Be sure to capture your thoughts.

✴ What is my ultimate goal and deepest desire in life? <u>Truth Time</u>: Deep down inside, is my ultimate goal or desire in life to avoid pain, or to bring glory to God?

LOOKING UPWARD ... A QUESTION TO TAKE TO GOD

When you ask God a question, expect His Spirit to respond to your heart. Be careful not to rush it, or manufacture an answer. Don't jot down your idea of the "right answer." Don't turn the Bible into a reference book or spiritual encyclopedia. Just pose the question to God, and wait on Him to speak personally in a fresh way. The litmus test for anything we hear from God is alignment with the Bible as our ultimate truth source. Always write down what you hear from God.

✴ God, how are my expectations of You realistic or unrealistic? How do You feel about my expectations?

Looking Forward ... Prepare for Session 7:

Please capture your thoughts and feelings in the "My Goals & Relationship Journal" on the next, page as you work through your healing process. Consider these questions that will be discussed in Session 7:

1. When do you feel the loneliest?
   ❒ In the mornings
   ❒ Meals at home
   ❒ Meals in restaurants
   ❒ On weekends
   ❒ Friday and/or Saturday nights
   ❒ In the evening
   ❒ At bedtime
   ❒ Sunday afternoons
   ❒ During holidays
   ❒ When around couples
   ❒ When watching Hallmark commercials
   ❒ Other: _____

2. Which of the following statements do you identify with the most?
   ❒ Loneliness feels like an icy wind
   ❒ Loneliness feels like a dull headache
   ❒ Loneliness haunts with memories of intimacy
   ❒ Loneliness feels empty like a vacant house
   ❒ Loneliness taunts with hopes of new intimacy
   ❒ Loneliness echoes in an empty apartment
   ❒ Loneliness clouds a sunny day
   ❒ Loneliness is a stalker that follows me everywhere
   ❒ Other: _____

3. The thought of dating or the prospect of a new relationship...
   ❒ Frightens me
   ❒ Intrigues me
   ❒ Repulses me
   ❒ Agitates me
   ❒ Interests me
   ❒ Bores me
   ❒ Excites me
   ❒ Confuses me
   ❒ Other: _____

My Goals & Relationship Journal

LONELINESS AND NEW RELATIONSHIPS

BREAKING THE ICE – 15 MINUTES

> LEADER: *The "Breaking the Ice" questions for this session focus on our desire for intimate companionship. They encourage people to consider what they value in friends.*

1. When you were in high school, which of the following groups did you wish you could've been accepted by?
   - ❏ The jocks
   - ❏ The computer geeks
   - ❏ The cheerleading squad
   - ❏ The choir or band
   - ❏ The popular girls
   - ❏ Other: _____

2. Through an unusual sequence of events you become the close friend and confidant of a well-known public figure (entertainment, sports, literature, arts, religion, government, business, etc.). What person would you choose to be this celebrity friend who trusts and confides in you? Why are you drawn to that person?

3. Describe the loneliest moment you ever experienced. What happened? Why did you feel so alone?

4. We've all come to know each other pretty well over these six session together. We all know there's not anything like a perfect person in this group. Would you be willing to share what you learned about your ultimate goal or deepest desire in your "Truth Time" this week?

5. Did you hear from God this week about your expectations of Him and of life?

6. In your take-home assignment, how did you respond to the thought of dating or the prospect of a new relationship? Please explain.

OPENING PRAYER

God, we wish that You were visible and physical, able to hold us in the dark, and sit with us in crowds. We miss loving and being loved. We miss having someone make us feel special. Holy Spirit, help us to feel Your loving presence tonight.

In the previous session we tried to make sense out of suffering and realized that difficulty is part of our landscape. We seek exemption or at least prompt relief from pain, but such expectations usually go unmet. God promises to meet us wherever we are on the journey and in whatever condition we find ourselves. He is a "very present help in times of trouble" (Psalm 46:1). In today's session, we'll discover that engaging the problem of loneliness and the issue of new relationships are an integral part of our healing journeys.

OBJECTIVES FOR THIS SESSION:
* Acknowledge the reality of loneliness
* Recognize the legitimate need for companionship and intimacy
* Accept the offer of Christian community
* Exercise caution in the pursuit of romantic relationships

DISCOVERING THE TRUTH – 30 MINUTES

LEADER: *In the initial part of "Discovering the Truth," you will examine some Scripture that explains that we are not meant to live life alone. Ask for volunteers to read the Scripture passages as you come to them. After this, you'll discuss some divorce dating cautions, and fulfilling our deepest desires. Keep things moving at a steady pace through "Discovering the Truth" and "Embracing the Truth." Leave ample time for the "Connecting" time.*

BY DESIGN

⁸ There was a man all alone; he had neither son nor brother. There was no end to his toil, yet his eyes were not content with his wealth. "For whom am I toiling," he asked, "and why am I depriving myself of enjoyment?" This too is meaningless—a miserable business.
⁹ Two are better than one, because they have a good return for their work: ¹⁰ If one falls down, his friend can help him up. But pity the man who falls and has no one to help him up.
¹¹ Also, if two lie down together, they will keep warm. But how can one keep warm alone?
¹² Though one may be overpowered one person, two can defend themselves. A cord of three strands is not quickly broken.

ECCLESIASTES 4:8-12 (NIV)

Then the Lord God said, "It is not good for the man to be alone. I will make a helper who is like him."

GENESIS 2:18 (HCSB)

1. What initially strikes you about this Ecclesiastes passage? What theme or phrase jumps out at you?

2. What does Genesis 2:18 say to you about how God feels about isolation and loneliness? What similarity do you see between God's declaration in Genesis and the statements made by the writer of Ecclesiastes?

In divorce, there's a tension between two truths. The first truth is that you are a whole person even though you are not married anymore. An unmarried person, whether never married or single again, is not half a person. You are not dependent upon another person for your validation. The second truth is that God created you for intimate relationship with another person. He designed you to long for companionship.

3. Since your divorce, how do you feel about your value as a woman or a man? How has the divorce affected your perception?

QUICK SHOPPERS

Divorced adults often lean to one of two extreme responses concerning the matter of new relationships. They either begin to believe that all men or women are villains to be avoided, or they begin to desperately need a man or woman in their lives. If you are currently very resistant to the idea of a new relationship and the thought of dating makes you nauseous, it's okay. That's where you are in the healing journey. Just be cautious not to categorically condemn the entire species of men or women. It may be how you feel, but it's not a fair or accurate assessment of the heart of all men or women.

If your resistance creates caution, that's a good thing. Regardless of what you currently feel about your own future prospects, the majority of divorced adults remarry. Unfortunately, many divorced adults date prematurely, and often are no more discerning than they were in their pre-divorce relationship. Newly single adults often have shorter courtships with brief (if any) engagement periods. Their logic tends to be that they are wiser as a result of their divorce, so they really know what they're looking for. A paraphrase of this thinking is. "I'm a smarter shopper, so I can shop quickly."

4. What do you see as a problem with that line of reasoning?

PREMATURE INTIMACY

There is a unique dating ritual among divorced adults that often accelerates the relationship and short-circuits rational discernment. On a first date, single again adults often share war stories from their divorces. They mutually disclose at a deep level. Often the silent and subtle response of both is, "You were mistreated. You are a victim just like me. You understand me and I understand you."

It's a powerful and intoxicating thing to be accepted and understood by a person of the opposite sex, especially if they are reasonably attractive and think you are too. Communication is a bridge to intimacy, and divorced adults have the capacity to build a bridge overnight. Mutual disclosure at a deep level creates a sense of closeness within both persons. This is not necessarily negative. Same gender friendships develop the same way. The problem in divorced dating is that this disclosure often goes too deep too early. The bridge is built, familiar and wonderful feelings stir again, and the couple frequently crosses the bridge to sexual expression and/or conversations about marriage prematurely.

FULFILLING OUR DEEPEST DESIRES

In John 4:1-26, Jesus encounters the Samaritan woman at the well. She has been married several times and is currently living with a man who is not her husband. Let's consider this discussion about quenching our deepest thirsts:

> LEADER: *To make reading this passage more interesting, you may opt to have a three people read the parts of Narrator, Jesus, and the Samaritan woman.*

NARRATOR: *⁷ A woman, a Samaritan came to draw water.*

JESUS: *Jesus said, "Would you give me a drink of water?" ⁸ (His disciples had gone to the village to buy food for lunch.)*

WOMAN: *⁹ The Samaritan woman, taken aback, asked, "How come You, a Jew, are asking me, a Samaritan woman, for a drink?" (Jews in those days wouldn't be caught dead talking to Samaritans.)*

JESUS: *¹⁰ Jesus answered, "If you knew the generosity of God, and who I am, you would be asking me for a drink, and I would give you fresh, living water."*

WOMAN: *¹¹ The woman said, "Sir, you don't even have a bucket to draw with, and this well is deep. So how are you you going to get this 'living water'? ¹² Are you a better man than our ancestor Jacob, who dug this well and drank from it, he and his sons and livestock, and have passed it on to us?"*

JESUS: *¹³ Jesus said, "Everyone who drinks this water will get thirsty again and again. ¹⁴ Anyone who drinks the water I give will never thirst—not ever The water I give will be an artesian spring within, gushing fountains of endless life."*

WOMAN: *¹⁵ The woman said "Sir, give me this water so I won't ever get thirsty, won't ever have to come back to this well again!"*

JOHN 4:7-15 (THE MESSAGE)

5. What is the Samaritan woman's strategy to fill her void?

6. What does her strategy reveal about her deep need?

7. How do we know her plan isn't working?

8. What to make of the fact that Jesus didn't exhort the woman to "curb" or squash her desires?

9. What does Jesus offer this multiple-divorced woman as a solution to her deepest need? What exactly is He offering (verses 13-14)?

The "living water" mentioned here is more than salvation. Too often we make salvation and the promise of heaven the answer to everything. Jesus offers the woman at the well "living water" to sooth her parched throat and quench her "living thirst" now. Heaven is not excluded, but heaven is not her immediate and deepest need. The fulfillment of her heart's great search is finding meaning and authentic love now.

[God speaking in metaphor:] For My people have committed a double evil: They have abandoned Me, the fountain of living water, and dug cisterns for themselves, cracked cisterns that cannot hold water.

JEREMIAH 2:13 (HCSB)

10. What does Jeremiah 2:13 say about our attempts to meet our own needs?

11. How does it go when we dig our own "cisterns"? How is your own digging going so far as you relay on your own resources to quench your deepest thirsts? Please explain.

Mobilizing Needed Support

The decision we need to make is not merely a choice between solitude and dating. Again, God understands our need for companionship. Divorce can be a time when we rediscover the value of friendships, and discover the gift of authentic Christian community. During the season of divorce, it's imperative that we mobilize supportive friendships. Every encounter does not have to include a serious, therapeutic discussion. Sometimes we just need a distraction and a break. Go with friends to a movie, a concert, or a coffeehouse with no other agenda than to laugh.

There is a point where we cross the border from healthy and necessary solitude into the lowlands of loneliness. During your moments of great loneliness or great struggle, reach out! Don't wait for someone to call you or expect others to read your mind, body language, mood, or facial expression. Initiate contact and request connection. God does not expect you to make it on your own. He didn't design you that way.

EMBRACING THE TRUTH – 25 Minutes

In addressing the problem of loneliness and considering the possibility of new relationships, you must recognize and accept the current season of your healing journey. Your position in the journey right now may dictate that dating would be premature, a form of pain avoidance, or an attempt to replace what or who you lost. If any of these are the case, you may need to acknowledge that it would not be fair to someone else to involve them in a close relationship in your current condition of emotional rehab.

1. How open are you to dating? How desperate to date would your friends and family say you are? How do you know if you're ready to date?

Friends and/or family may tell you, "You should get in the game again. You ought to start dating." If you're not ready, don't be coerced or pressured into dating. On the other hand, a desperate need to date should raise a red flag. Feeling ready and open, but with a healthy dose of caution, is a sign of readiness. Being resistant to dating or being overly eager to date is an indicator of unfinished business, and a signal that you should postpone dating until those issues are adequately addressed.

2. If you have children, how are they dealing with the divorce? How ready do you think
   they are for you to start dating?

Children should not be permitted to control your life. However, as a general rule, your dating should not cause trauma for your kids. If you have more than one child, each one will have a different reaction to the prospect or the reality of you introducing a romantic partner into your life (and theirs). An older child may tell you, "Go for it, Mom!" while a younger child sends signals of resistance. A single parent must be sensitive to a child's place in the healing journey. Consider the child's age, maturity, personality, level of closeness to you, and degree of attachment to the other parent. Except in extreme situations, children usually hope for a reconciliation of their parents. Parental sensitivity takes into account their children's level of healing and the stubbornness of their hope.

As you prepare yourself to date, consider these three vital qualities of a healthy relationship ...

CHARACTER

Do not be mismatched with unbelievers. For what partnership is there between righteousness and lawlessness? Or what fellowship does light have with darkness?

2 CORINTHIANS 6:14 (HCSB)

3. What does Paul warn us about in 2 Corinthians 6:14? Why would God give us this
   instruction?

4. What character qualities should I bring to a healthy relationship? What qualities am I looking for in someone else?

Christ-centered relationships work when people take responsibility for their behavior, confess their own failures, and seek to grow in Christ. A Christian marriage isn't merely a romantic merger of two church attendees. It is a bonding of two adults who are genuine God-worshipers and Christ-followers. This is the ultimate cord of three strands (two adults and God) that influences character. Make sure you are assessing your partner's character based on current evidence and not future potential. "He has potential" is a flimsy excuse for overlooking character issues. Your partner's closest friends are another good character gauge. Our closest friendships reveal something of our values because we are drawn to people whose values are similar to our own.

COMPATIBILITY

Similarities in a relationship are like deposits, and differences are like withdrawals. In a relationship, similarities reveal compatibility. Differences in themselves are not crippling. We are not looking for an exact replica of ourselves in a different-sex model. However, the more you have in common with your partner, the better your chances are for long-term stability and satisfaction.

5. In 2 Corinthians 6:14, spiritual and directional compatibility are identified as the central issue. In any future relationship, what are my non-negotiables—the key areas of compatibility where we must see eye to eye? (Examples: values, faith, goals, marriage, family, and so on.)

COMMUNICATION

25 Therefore, laying aside falsehood, speak truth each one of you with his neighbor, for we are members of one another. 26 Be angry, and yet do not sin; do not let the sun go down on your anger, 27 and do not give the devil an opportunity. ... 29 Let no unwholesome [Literally rotten] word proceed from your mouth, but only such a word as is good for edification according to the need of the moment, so that it will give grace to those who hear.

EPHESIANS 4:25-27,29 (NASB)

6. What can be the results of poor communication in future relationships?

7. Was communication a problem in your marriage? Which areas of communication would you need to grow in for the sake of any future relationship?

Healthy relationships are characterized by good communication on three levels: disclosure, negotiation, and conflict-resolution.

(1) The disclosure level involves a mutual sharing of ourselves. Communication in this level involves sharing our thoughts, feelings, beliefs, opinions, experiences, preferences, hopes, dreams, fears, and goals.

(2) Communication in the negotiation level involves decision making. A couple's negotiation style reveals how they share power, and make decisions in the relationship. Negotiation is required for minor issues (Which restaurant and movie are we going to?) as well as major issues (Are we going to relocate because you got a job offer?). The ability to negotiate is a vital component of a healthy relationship.

(3) Finally, communication in the conflict-resolution level requires an ability to work through a disagreement or problem. The evidence of effective conflict-resolution communication is resolved issues and restored relationships.

CONNECTING – 20 MINUTES

LEADER INSTRUCTIONS FOR GROUP EXPERIENCE: You will need a LARGE BALL OF UNBROKEN STRING OR YARN for this exercise. It might be wise to have two, just in case you need to attach them. Have group members form a standing circle. The object of this exercise is to pass the ball of string or yarn around so that a "line" connects each group member. This part of the exercise is complete when each participant is holding lines that connect him or her to all the other group members. The group's challenge is to determine how to accomplish this task and make it work. ...

When the exercise is successfully completed, there should be the appearance of a web. Explain that this web illustrates the WEB OF CARE that exists in the group. Remind the group that they all came into the study with their own hurts, issues, and needs that needed to be healed. This group has just clearly illustrated Philippians 2:4:

"Everyone should look out not only for his own interests, but also for the interests of others."

Explanation of the "Web of Care": In this group, we have *not* avoided our own issues by focusing on our neighbor's problems. Rather, part of our own healing has been to enter into and understand someone else's pain by supporting and encouraging him or her.

Poet Kahlil Gibran writes, "You may forget with whom you have laughed but not with whom you have wept." Over the past weeks, we have laughed and cried together. This "Web of Care" is a reminder that we are not on this journey alone. We are connected, and in this journey together.

1. Take turns responding to the following questions: How has this group helped and supported you on your healing journey? What has God revealed to you in this session?

LEADER PRAYER OPTION: *Page 125 shows a music CD:* Pursued by God: Redemptive Worship Volume 1 *from Serendipity House. In place of your group prayer time, you may want to play the two songs "I Worship You" and More" from that CD. Download lyrics from www.SerendipityHouse.com/Community (under Group Leaders - Practical Tools). Ask group members to close their eyes and listen, or follow along with the printed lyrics (if they prefer). At the end of the song privately respond back to God.*

MY PRAYER REQUESTS:

MY GROUP'S PRAYER REQUESTS:

In addition to specific prayer requests, thank God for bringing each individual to join this group and for the experiences you have shared together.

Taking It Home

Looking Inward ... A Question to Take to My Heart:

Look into your heart for the answer to these questions. This is introspection time—time to grapple with what drives your thinking and behavior. <u>Every action has a corresponding belief that drives it.</u> Dig for what you believe in the deep recesses of your heart about God, yourself, and the world in which you live. Be sure to capture your thoughts.

⁕ Do I have a close friend or two in town that I could call for any reason at any time of the day or night? If not, what is preventing me from developing close friendships?

Looking Upward ... A Question to Take to God

When you ask God a question, expect His Spirit to respond to your heart. Be careful not to rush it, or manufacture an answer. Don't jot down your idea of the "right answer." Don't turn the Bible into a reference book or spiritual encyclopedia. Just pose the question to God, and wait on Him to speak personally in a fresh way. The litmus test for anything we hear from God is alignment with the Bible as our ultimate truth source. Always write down what you hear from God.

⁕ God, You created me with the longing for intimacy and companionship. How do You want to meet that need during this season of my life? What do You want to tell me about future relationships and dating? About remarriage?

LOOKING FORWARD ... PREPARE FOR SESSION 8:

Please capture your thoughts and feelings on the "Contentment Journal" on the next page, as you continue on this healing journey. Consider these questions that will be discussed in Session 8:

1. How would you rate your present level of contentment?

1...........2...........3...........4...........5...........6...........7...........8...........9...........10

Life Stinks!   It's Been Better   No Complaints   Content   Life's Great!

2. If you were sent to prison, like the Apostle Paul was, for being a fervent Christian, what do you think your attitude would be?
   - ❒ So, this is the reward for following Christ?!
   - ❒ This jail stinks; this food stinks; these guards really stink; I stink; life stinks!
   - ❒ I should have remained a Pharisee.
   - ❒ I'll suffer through it.
   - ❒ I want to call my lawyer.
   - ❒ I'd rather die than be stuck in here.
   - ❒ With God's help, I'll survive one day at a time.
   - ❒ I love Jesus, but He must not love me!
   - ❒ These conditions are worse than *Survivor*!
   - ❒ Other: _____

3. With which of the following are you <u>discontented</u>? Check all that apply.
   - ❒ Career
   - ❒ Finances
   - ❒ Housing
   - ❒ Geography
   - ❒ Singleness
   - ❒ Marriage
   - ❒ Parenting/Children
   - ❒ Childlessness
   - ❒ Physical Health
   - ❒ Physical Appearance
   - ❒ Car
   - ❒ Leisure Time
   - ❒ Friendships
   - ❒ Other:_____

Contentment Journal

FINDING A NEW PATH TO CONTENTMENT

BREAKING THE ICE – 15 MINUTES

LEADER: At the beginning of the session, inform the group that during this final session you've got a surprise treat for them—"a delicious dessert and beverage" to be served after everyone gets settled in.

1. When you were a teenager, what was the most exciting vacation or excursion you ever experienced? Which of the following best describes what made it so special for you?
   - ❏ I didn't know what was coming next. Every moment was an exciting, surprising adventure.
   - ❏ We visited places I'd never been before.
   - ❏ I was in a new environment, one that I quickly learned to appreciate and enjoy.
   - ❏ I was with my family or friends, people I enjoyed being with.
   - ❏ I learned new skills that I take pleasure in to this day.
   - ❏ Other: _____

2. When you were a child, who was the "hero" in your story? What did they do to deserve that title?

3. Which of the following best describes where you are on life's journey right now?
   - ❏ Y in the Road – I know if I'm going to be whole, I need to choose the right path and go forward.
   - ❏ Stuck in the Mud – I won't stop trying, but I feel like I'm still spinning my wheels.
   - ❏ End of the Road – I've lost my passion for the journey. I've done all I can do, and I don't know where else to turn.
   - ❏ Lost – I'm moving forward no matter what, but I don't know what to do next.
   - ❏ Backtracking – I tend to find myself reliving difficult experiences, and when I do I keep myself from finding my phenomenal future.
   - ❏ Other: _____

4. How did your "Taking It Home" assignments go? Would you share a key insight that you gained from the question you took to your heart or the question you asked of God bout friendships or dating?

5. Hopefully you spent some time considering the topic of contentment as part of your homework. How would you describe your present level of contentment?

Opening Prayer

God, how can we possibly be content with divorce? The whole concept of contentment just doesn't make sense to us, but we're listening. Help us to listen to Your challenging but gentle message, and your correcting but reassuring voice.

Have you ever looked at what was happening in your life and said, "How did I get here? This isn't where I wanted to be. This isn't what I planned for." Some of you feel like that. You worked hard, remained faithful, and prayed fervently. You pressed the button for "Good Marriage" and instead got "Divorce." Disappointment, grief, and even anger are the result.

This is our final session in *Recovering from Divorce*. We're making progress, but our grief is not over, our disappointment is not wiped away, our worries have not been eliminated, and our anger has not evaporated. So, how do we move on in this season of our lives? In this session, we're going to examine a life of contentment versus a life of discontentment. Clearly, we all long for contentment.

Objectives For This Session:
- Understand that contentment, according to the Apostle Paul, is a learned behavior
- Recognize that contentment does not dwell on comparisons or depend on circumstance
- Accept disappointment, but not despair
- Learn to celebrate the special people and moments in our lives

> LEADER: Say, "There are often wonderful things about the past that we miss, and there are exciting possibilities in the future that we long for. Yet, it is possible to get stuck lamenting what is no more, or resenting what may never happen. Discontentment holds today's joy hostage with a list of demands of how things ought to be."

DISCOVERING THE TRUTH – 35 MINUTES

> LEADER: *In the initial part of "Discovering the Truth," you'll examine the topic of unfulfilled expectations. Ask for volunteers to read various Scripture passages as you come to them. After this, you will discover the meaning of contentment by studying Paul's definition. Keep things moving at a steady pace through "Discovering the Truth" and "Embracing the Truth." Leave time for the "Connecting" time.*

UNFULFILLED EXPECTATIONS

> LEADER: *Excuse yourself to get the "treats" and return with a box of saltine crackers, paper cups, and a gallon of water. Without explaining, have everyone eat a saltine cracker and drink some water. Then ask the following questions:*

1. What was it like to anticipate a delicious dessert and be served crackers and water? What were some of your thoughts and feelings?

2. In what ways does this experience remind you of the disappointment of divorce?

[Written by Paul] I rejoiced in the Lord greatly that now at last you have renewed your concern for me. You were, in fact, concerned about me, but lacked the opportunity to show it. I don't say this out of need, for I have learned to be content in whatever circumstances I am. I know both how to have a little, and I know how to have a lot. In any and all circumstances I have learned the secret of being content—whether well-fed or hungry, whether in abundance or in need. I am able to do all things through Him who strengthens me.

PHILIPPIANS 4:10-13 (HCSB)

If you find contentment illusive, or if you struggle with unfulfilled expectations then meditate on Paul's remarkable attitude in the midst of unfulfilled hopes. Paul is a worthy mentor on the subject of contentment. He had hoped to go to Rome to tell people about Jesus. Instead, he found himself locked up as a prisoner.

3. What would your reaction be if you were in Paul's place? How can he really be content?

COMMON MISCONCEPTIONS

Blessed are those who mourn, because they will be comforted.

MATTHEW 5:4 (HCSB)

We are pressured in every way but not crushed; we are perplexed but not in despair.

2 CORINTHIANS 4:8 (HCSB)

4. Does being content mean that we don't feel or that we live above the fray? Explain your thoughts.

5. In Matthew 5:4, Jesus encourages us to grieve but, in 2 Corinthians, Paul says that we are not to despair. What's the difference?

6. I'm especially relieved that contentment ... (Check all that apply)
   ❑ Does not mean that I have to give up my hopes, goals, or dreams
   ❑ Does not mean that I cannot wish things were different
   ❑ Does not mean that I should never be disappointed or angry
   ❑ Does not mean I can't grieve what might have been
   ❑ Other: _____

Before we examine what contentment is, let's first discover what it's NOT. Contentment is not complacency. Being content does not mean that we don't pursue goals or work for change. To have a vision means that we can see and describe a preferable future. Being content does not mean that we don't have a preference about how things should turn out. If Paul had been given the option of staying in jail or getting out, what do you think he would have chosen? Secondly, contentment allows for disappointment. Being content in a situation does not mean that we do not grieve what might have been. Instead, contentment means that we're not immobilized by despair when life strays from the script we wrote for it.

The Comparison Trap

Most people are led into discontentment when they begin the comparison game. Let's consider three deadly comparisons:

COMPARISON I: What I have vs. What I should have

Each person should remain in the life situation in which he was called.

1 CORINTHIANS 7:20 (HCSB)

Cease striving and know that I am God; I will be exalted among the nations, I will be exalted in the earth.

PSALM 46:10 (NASB)

7. In both of these verses, what is the point relative to discontentment?

This comparison causes us to obsess about what we want, need, or "deserve. Calvin Miller says, "When we focus on how things ought to be, the oughtness can be so consuming it steals our peace. To cover our absentee peace we prefer to say that we are burdened rather than worried. But our word games do not conceal the truth. We are uncomfortable with the moment. We live well for how things ought to be but not so well with how things are. The whole key to living in happiness is our ability to disentangle ourselves from ought-ness until we have peace with is-ness."

8. Have you ever fallen into the trap of comparison I? Have you ever thought, "I'm divorced, but I should be married"? How does this type of thinking steal our peace?

COMPARISON 2: What I have now vs. What I once had and lost

Therefore since we also have such a large cloud of witnesses surrounding us, let us lay aside every weight and the sin that so easily ensnares us, and run with endurance the race that lies before us,

HEBREWS 12:1 (HCSB)

Brothers, I do not consider myself yet to have taken hold of it. But one thing I do: Forgetting what is behind and straining toward what is ahead, I press on ...

PHILIPPIANS 3:13-14A (NIV)

9. What happens to a runner in a race when he's always looking back, focused on where he's been (Hebrews 12:1 and Philippians 3:13-14)?

10. What is Paul's advice in Philippians 3? What do you think he means by "forgetting"? What do you think he isn't trying to say by use the word "forgetting"?

As a Pharisee, Paul had known status, wealth, and comfort. While he was in jail, he did not contrast his present condition to his pre-conversion life of ease. He gives us a perfect example of how not to fall into this comparison trap. Remember, we should grieve our losses, and times of reviewing the past are critical to our progress. But, we can't stay focused on what has been lost, and what could have been. Dwelling in the past, and obsessing about what we once had will sabotage our contentment.

11. Have you ever fallen into the trap of comparison 2? Have you ever thought, "I'm divorced now, but I was happily married once"? In what ways does this type of thinking sabotage our contentment?

COMPARISON 3: What I have vs. What others have

But godliness actually is a means of great gain when accompanied by contentment.

1 TIMOTHY 6:6 (NASB)

12. What is the benefit of fighting off discontentment according to 1 Timothy?

Contentment is undermined by comparisons. We can always find people who are more attractive, wealthier, and more successful than we are. There will always be people who seem to enjoy more freedoms, better relationships, and fewer problems than we do. "Their SUV is newer, their complexion is better, and their children are better behaved. They have dream jobs, few health problems, and take incredible vacations." But, when our eyes are on what everyone else has, we miss the blessings and the joys that God has given us. This comparison trap robs us of the gift of life God has blessed us with.

13. Have you ever fallen into the trap of comparison 3? Have you ever thought, "I'm divorced, but others are happily married"? In what ways does this type of thinking rob us of our joy?

EMBRACING THE TRUTH – 25 MINUTES

PAUL'S REMARKABLE CONTENTMENT

Paul claims to have learned to be content "whatever the circumstances." If Paul had been writing about unconditional contentment from a comfy office in Philippi, it would be easy for us to respond, "Sure, Paul. How about test driving my life for a few laps, and then we'll see how content you are!"

But Paul's declaration of contentment silences our sarcasm, because it echoes off of our prison walls. We may feel trapped by divorce, or imprisoned by some other undesirable circumstances. Paul was chained to Roman soldiers 24 hours a day, yet he was not held captive by discontentment. Neither did he feel tortured by his circumstances. Perhaps you can't identify with that kind of victory. At the very least, allow this session to spur you on to search and discover Paul's secret.

Paul's extraordinary attitude comes from his remarkable perspective on life. In Philippians, Paul writes that he believes:
- God's glory is more important than his comfort or success (1:20, 2:16-17)
- His citizenship is not here in this world (3:20)
- This world cannot contain his highest ambition (3:7-8)
- What other people think of him is not of the highest importance (1:15-18)

1. Which of these four perspectives do you long for the most? Why?

Paul's secret to being content is that he understands that contentment is a learned behavior. Paul says, "I've learned to be content whatever the circumstance," and "I've learned the secret of being content." Don't think that some people just have the personality and the natural capacity to be content and others don't. If you know anything about Paul, he was not a laid-back kind of guy—he was very intense. He was goal-oriented and very passionate. Paul was not naturally content—he *learned* contentment. Let's examine the lessons Paul learned that contributed to his contentment:

(1) Paul learned to trust God's goodness. He did not measure God's goodness according to favorable circumstances.

(2) Paul learned to find meaning in the midst of difficulty. His imprisonment gave him the opportunity to share the story of Jesus' death and resurrection with the Roman guards. Paul's life exemplifies the saying, "Suffering is difficult—suffering without meaning is intolerable."

(3) Paul learned to find cause for celebration. He celebrated his relationship with the Philippians, and rejoiced that his imprisonment served to ignite their boldness.

2. Which of these statements is the most true for you personally? Discuss ways to grow.
   ❏ I need to learn to trust God's goodness.
   ❏ I need to learn to find meaning in the midst of difficulty.
   ❏ I need to learn to find causes for celebration.

LEADER: Say, "We're going to connect the ancient writings of Paul with a contemporary reading from Emily Kingsley, a mother of a child with a birth defect." Then, read this story from Kingsley aloud to the group (as quoted by Pam Vredvelt in Espresso for The Spirit, Multnomah, 1996.).

I am often asked to describe the experience of raising a child with a disability—to try to help people who have not shared that unique experience to understand it, to imagine how it would feel. It's like this ...

When you're going to have a baby, it's like planning a fabulous vacation trip to Italy. You buy a bunch of guidebooks and make your wonderful plans. The Coliseum. The Michelangelo David. The gondolas in Venice. You may learn some handy phrases in Italian. It's all very exciting.

After months of eager anticipation, the day finally arrives. You pack your bags and off you go. Several hours later, the plane lands. The stewardess comes in and says, "Welcome to Holland."

"Holland?!?" you say. "What do you mean Holland? I signed up for Italy! I'm supposed to be in Italy. All my life I've dreamed of going to Italy."

But there's been a change in the flight plan. They've landed in Holland and there you must stay.

The important thing is that they haven't taken you to a horrible, disgusting, filthy place, full of pestilence, famine and disease. It's just a different place.

So you must go out and buy new guide books. And you must learn a whole new language. And you will meet a whole new group of people you would never have met.

It's just a different place. It's slower-paced than Italy, less flashy than Italy. But after you've been there for a while and you catch your breath, you look around ... and you begin to notice that Holland has windmills ... and Holland has tulips. Holland even has Rembrandts.

But everyone you know is busy coming and going from Italy ... and they're all bragging about what a wonderful time they had there. And for the rest of your life, you will say, "Yes, that's where I was supposed to go. That's what I had planned."

And the pain of that will never, ever, go completely away ... because the loss of that dream is a very significant loss.

But ... if you spend your life mourning the fact that you didn't get to Italy, you may never be free to enjoy the very special, the very lovely things ... about Holland.

You don't have a child with a disability in order to relate to this story. Your Italy was a happy marriage, and Holland is being single again. No one expects you to walk out your front door every morning and say, "Isn't it a beautiful day? I just love being divorced!" Being content in Holland is not celebrating divorce. It's learning to accept your circumstances and live life fully (and contentedly) in spite of them.

3. Finish this sentence:

I think as it relates to being single again, being content in Holland for me means ...

LESSONS FROM EMILY KINGSLEY AND THE APOSTLE PAUL

LESSON 1: You don't have to pretend that you're not disappointed with a profound loss.

If you wind up in Holland instead of Italy, you'll be disappointed. Remember that contentment allows for disappointment, but it does not give in to immobilizing despair. Author and counselor John Eldredge says, "Being content is not pretending that everything is the way you wish it would be; it is not acting as though you have no wishes. Rather, it is no longer being ruled by your desires."

4. What is the one thing that you are most disappointed about concerning your divorce?

LESSON 2: You must learn a new language.

You must to learn to be present in your "now." Go ahead and grieve, but determine to learn a new language of contentment in this foreign territory. If you get stuck in the comparison trap, you're not learning the new language. Insisting that you can't be happy because or unless (you name it) happens is the emergence of your accent from the old dialect. Remember, Paul had to learn to be content—it didn't come naturally or quickly to him.

5. What will you do to begin to learn this new language in the foreign culture you're in?

LESSON 3: You must find special people, places, and moments to celebrate.

Holland has windmills, tulips, and Rembrandts. Paul extracted positive outcomes from his undesirable situation, and recognized new possibilities (Philippians 1:12-14). You can become fixated on what's wrong or missing from your Holland station of life, or you can become a tourist and an explorer of this place and season you're in. There are existing relationships to appreciate, and new ones to pursue. There are unique places, things, events, moments, and opportunities that await you.

6. To which of these principles of contentment will you need to give extra attention as you move forward?
   ❑ I don't have to pretend that I'm not disappointed with my profound loss.
   ❑ I must learn a new language for a foreign culture.
   ❑ I must find special people, places, and moments to celebrate.

CONNECTING – 15 MINUTES

LEADER INSTRUCTIONS FOR GROUP EXPERIENCE:

MOVIE CLIP:

For this exercise, you will need a DVD of the film Polar Express. *Most of your group members will have either read the children's book, seen the movie, or both. Show the scene toward the movie's conclusion in which the conductor punches the children's tickets as they prepare to board the train back home. Each child's ticket discloses a character quality revealed in the story, and also affirmed by the conductor.*

AFFIRMATION CARDS:

This is going to be a very meaningful and powerful moment for the group members. Give everyone in the group (yourself included) an index card. Have everyone put their names at the top of their cards. Then, have group members pass their cards to the right. Beneath the person's name, each group member who receives the card will write one affirming word *that describes that person's character, strength, or growth. You may want to give some examples like Perseverance, Caring, Humor, Courageous, Kind-hearted, Resilient, and Inspiring. Ask people, if possible, to avoid duplicating someone else's descriptive word. Continue passing the cards around, and inscribing them until each member has his or her own index card again ... now filled with affirming words.*

Ask the members to take turns reading the words on their cards aloud. You begin. For some, this may be an emotional moment. That's okay. After everyone has finished reading, ask the group to describe how it feels to see those affirming words on their cards.

GROUP NEXT STEPS:

At the end of this experience, the group members will feel a close sense of connection. At the same time, they are aware that this is the final session. Depending upon your own plans for the group and/or whether the group plans to continue to meet and study another series, you must be sensitive to what degree and sense of closure the group needs. Choose one or more of the following options ...

OPTION 1: This would be a good time to suggest to the group that redemptive community has had time to take root in your meetings together. Remind them that their journeys are only beginning. Ask the group if they would consider keeping the group together for continued support and redemption. Pass around 3 x 5" cards so people can jot down their potential interest. Some of the group members may be open to the idea.

OPTION 2: Encourage group members to join the next Recovering from Divorce group, either to go through the process again at a deeper level, or to take to an active role in helping to lead the group as a mentor, small-group facilitator, accountability partner, or some other job that fits well (discuss the potential with the group facilitator).

OPTION 3: If there are not enough to form a small group, refer these people to your pastor to connect them with a group. If you form a group that does not want to go through Recovering from Divorce again, we suggest your next step would be to go through the Serendipity House study entitled Great Beginnings. You may order this and other group resources online at www.SerendipityHouse.com.

OPTION 4: Some support groups like to meet in a month or so for a potluck dinner or a get-together at a restaurant. You may consider offering that as a recommendation. Knowing that a reunion is not far off may help many group members with today's study conclusion, especially if you don't plan to continue your group.

Share specific prayer needs. In addition to specific prayer requests, thank God for the hope and healing that He has been progressively revealing to each individual and to the group. Thank Him for His extravagant love!

LEADER PRAYER OPTION: Page 125 shows a music CD: Pursued by God: Redemptive Worship Volume 1 from Serendipity House. In place of your group prayer time, you may want to play the song "Royalty" from that CD. Download lyrics from www.SerendipityHouse.com/Community (under Group Leaders - Practical Tools). Ask group members to close their eyes and listen, or follow along with the printed lyrics (if they prefer). At the end of the song privately respond back to God.

MY PRAYER REQUESTS:

MY GROUP'S PRAYER REQUESTS:

TAKING IT HOME

A QUESTION TO TAKE TO GOD:

✳ God, how do You plan to redeem this season of pain and loss in my life? What do You want to tell me about where You want to take me?

Required Supplies and Preparation for Each Session

This section lists the supplies required for the Group Experiences in each session of the study. The procedural instructions for the experiences are also given within each session.

Session 1:

Supplies: - Candles for each group member (that don't drip hot wax)
- Large center candle
- Disposable lighter or matches

Procedure:
Pass candles out to everyone in the room. Dim the lights. Light a center candle on the floor or table and have everyone light their candles from the center flame. When all of the candles have been lit, have the group take a moment to notice the warmth and the glow of their own flame.

DISCUSS QUESTION 1. *Then, just before question 2, on your cue, have everyone blow their candles out. At this time, the group leader should reignite his/her candle from the center candle, which never went out. The leader will use his/her candle to re-light the candle of the group member closest to him/her. One by one, group members will "pass the flame" until all the candles are lit again.*

Once all of the candles are lit, say, "Jesus said, 'I am the light of the world. He who believes in Me will not walk in darkness.' The center candle never went out. From it we brought light and life back to our own candle. We also shared our flame with one another. God gives us Himself, and He gives us the gift of supportive friendships. Over the next several weeks, we'll regain our strength from God and receive support, acceptance, and encouragement from one another."

Session 2:

Supplies: - DVD player or Video cassette player and TV/Video system
- DVD of the movie *Castaway*

Procedure:
Have the TV/DVD player set up close by, and the Castaway DVD cued up to the scene where Tom Hank's character loses Wilson in the ocean. Show Scene 24 from 1:43:33 to 1:4457 minutes on the DVD. Verbally set the scene by reading the line that precedes question 1.

Session 3:

Supplies: - Full-size sheets of paper for each group member
            - Pens or pencils for each group member
            - Trash can

Procedure:

Distribute full-size sheets of blank paper, and pens or pencils to each group member. Instruct people to write down all of the things that their former spouse has done and is doing that makes them angry. Tell them to be candid, because they won't have to share anything on this paper.

Next, have them write down ways they might be frustrated or angry with God. Assure them that they won't be struck by lightning. God already knows their anger and can handle it. To get them thinking, use these examples:

- If You hate divorce then why didn't You save my marriage?
- Why are You letting my child(ren) suffer like this?
- Why am I suffering when he/she is the one that wrecked our marriage?
- You know the truth. Why did You let the judge approve that settlement or custody arrangement?

Encourage them to write down their frustrations with God, their questions, and their accusations. Assure them that they won't have to share these either.

When everyone is finished, have the group wad their papers up into a tight ball. Have them really squeeze it hard and notice the tension in their forearms and hands. Pass the trash can around. Have each member unfold his or her paper ball, rip it into shreds, and throw it into the trash can.

Session 4:

Supplies: - DVD player or Video cassette player and TV/Video system
            - DVD of the movie *Les Misérables*

Procedure:

Prior to the session, set up the TV/DVD player with the movie *Les Misérables*, starring Liam Neeson. Watch Scenes 2-4 (beginning just past the credits from 02:55 to 09:52 minutes on the DVD) through the dramatic close-up conversation between the priest and Jean Valjean after the priest gives Valjean the silver candlesticks. Then, have the group answer the questions.

SESSION 5:

Supplies: - 3 x 5" index cards for each group member
          - Pens or pencils for each group member

Procedure:
Pass out 3 x 5" index cards for Question 1. Then, using the Group Experience, illustrate that it's only normal to feel a sense of apprehension or holding back when under pressure.

Connecting Question 1:
Spend a minute or two scanning back through today's session. What was the most meaningful Scripture, principle, idea, or statement in this session for you personally? Write the meaning-ful thought on a 3 x 5" index card; keep it in visible spot at home.

Group Experience:
Be sensitive to each person's comfort level as you lead this experience. Have the group mem-bers gather around a seated member of the group and place their hands on the seated mem-ber's head, shoulders, and arms. Then, have the seated member try to stand up as the other group members attempt to prevent that from happening. Have the group offer resistance past the point of it being funny. The seated member should feel some frustration. Finally, have a group member extend a hand and help the seated member up. This process should be repeated so that every group member experiences the resistance followed the assistance to stand. When everyone has had a turn, answer the following questions as a group:

SESSION 6:

Supplies: - Each group member should bring a favorite mug or beverage container from home
          - *Pursued by God: Redemptive Worship* from Serendipity, or your own music CD
          - loaf or loaves of Italian or French bread
          - grape juice & extra mugs or cups for those who forgot to bring one

In preparation for this "Connecting" time, ask your group members beforehand to bring their favorite coffee mug or beverage container to this meeting. If you forgot to mention this at the end of last week's session, contact group members by phone or e-mail before this session and give them the simple assignment.

Procedure:
SHOW & TELL:
Ask the group members to display their mug or glass and answer these two questions:
     (1) "Why is this your favorite mug or glass?"
     (2) "What does this mug or glass say about you?"

... SESSION 6 CONTINUED:

If people forget to bring a mug, simply ask them to describe their favorite beverage container, and answer the questions. NOTE: You will need to bring extra mugs or cups to provide them for the communion time that's coming up.

Procedure:
LISTENING PRAYER TIME:
You're going to lead group members in a short time of listening prayer.
• Allow this experience some time; don't rush it.
• Put on quiet background music (use the CD *Pursued by God: Redemptive Worship Volume 1* from Serendipity House, or select your own music); dim the lights if possible.
• Help each person create a small personal area. This is not a time to chat; make it very honoring.
• Trust God to speak to each person individually.

Ask your group members to close their eyes, and envision Jesus sitting right here in the room. Then, read Hebrews 4:15-16 from *The Message* paraphrase of the Bible: "We don't have a priest who is out of touch with our reality. He's been through weakness and testing, experienced it all—all but the sin. So let's walk right up to him and get what he is so ready to give. Take the mercy, accept the help." Pause, and then instruct group members to:

1. Ask Jesus to show you how He feels about your struggles, your failures, and your pain.

2. Now ask Him how He feels about you.

3. Accept Jesus' mercy and help ... allow that burden of suffering and shame to lift off of you.

Procedure:
COMMUNION EXPERIENCE:

NOTE: *If you or your church leadership are uncomfortable with you leading the communion or Eucharist experience, be sure to invite your pastor, minister, priest or church leader to serve communion. This experience will most likely be one of the most meaningful moments in this series.*

Follow the procedure written in Session 6.

SESSION 7:
Supplies: - Two large ball of unbroken string or yarn
- OPTIONAL: *Pursued by God: Redemptive Worship* from Serendipity
- OPTIONAL: *Pursued by God* lyrics downloaded from Web

Procedure:

Have group members form a standing circle. The object of this exercise is to pass the ball of string or yarn around so that a "line" connects each group member. This part of the exercise is complete when each participant is holding lines that connect him or her to all the other group members. The group's challenge is to determine how to accomplish this task and make it work. ...

When the exercise is successfully completed, there should be the appearance of a web. Explain that this web illustrates the WEB OF CARE that exists in the group. Remind the group that they all came into the study with their own hurts, issues, and needs that needed to be healed. This group has just clearly illustrated Philippians 2:4:

> *"Everyone should look out not only for his own interests, but also for the interests of others."*

LEADER PRAYER OPTION:

Page 125 shows a music CD: *Pursued by God: Redemptive Worship Volume 1* from Serendipity House. In place of your group prayer time, you may want to play the two songs "I Worship You" and More" from that CD. Download lyrics from www.SerendipityHouse.com/Community (under Group Leaders - Practical Tools). Ask group members to close their eyes and listen, or follow along with the printed lyrics (if they prefer). At the end of the song privately respond back to God.

SESSION 8:

Supplies: - DVD player or Video cassette player and TV/Video system
- DVD of the *Polar Express*
- Index cards & pens for each group member
- OPTIONAL: *Pursued by God: Redemptive Worship* from Serendipity
- OPTIONAL: *Pursued by God* lyrics downloaded from Web

Procedure:

MOVIE CLIP:

Show the scene toward the movie's conclusion in which the conductor punches the children's tickets as they prepare to board the train back home. Each child's ticket discloses a character quality revealed in the story, and also affirmed by the conductor.

AFFIRMATION CARDS: Follow the procedure written in Session 6.

LEADER PRAYER OPTION:

Page 125 shows a music CD: *Pursued by God: Redemptive Worship Volume 1* from Serendipity House. In place of your group prayer time, you may want to play the song "Royalty" from that CD. Download lyrics from www.SerendipityHouse.com/Community (under Group Leaders - Practical Tools). Ask group members to close their eyes and listen, or follow along with the printed lyrics (if they prefer). At the end of the song privately respond back to God.

LEADING A SUCCESSFUL DIVORCE RECOVERY GROUP

You will find a great deal of helpful information in this section that will be crucial for success as you lead your group.

Reading through this and utilizing the suggested principles and practices will greatly enhance the group experience. You need to accept the limitations of leadership. You cannot transform a life. You must lead your group to the Bible, the Holy Spirit, and the power of Christian community. By doing so your group will have all the tools necessary to walk through the grieving process and embrace life and hope on the other side. The grief process normally lasts longer than eight weeks. But the connections that are built and the truths learned with allow your group members to move toward wholeness.

MAKE THE FOLLOWING THINGS AVAILABLE AT EACH SESSION
- *Recovering from Divorce: The Death of a Dream* book for each attendee
- Bible for each attendee
- Boxes of tissue
- Snacks and refreshments
- Dark chocolates
- Pens or pencils for each attendee

Most every session will demand other items be available. Check the list and make sure you have what is needed for each session.

THE SETTING

GENERAL TIPS:
1. Prepare for each meeting by reviewing the material, praying for each group member, asking the Holy Spirit to join you at each meeting, and making Jesus the centerpiece of every experience.

2. Create the right environment by making sure chairs are arranged so each person can see the eyes of every other attendee. Set the room temperature at 69 degrees. Make sure pets are in a location where they cannot interrupt the meeting. Request that cell phones are turned off unless someone is expecting an emergency call. Have music playing as people arrive (volume low enough for people to converse) and, if possible, burn a sweet-smelling candle.

3. Try to have soft drinks and coffee available for early arrivals.

4. Have someone with the spiritual gift of hospitality ready to make any new attendees feel welcome.

5. Be sure there is adequate lighting so that everyone can read without straining.

6. There are four types of questions used in each session: Observation (What is the passage telling us?), Interpretation (What does the passage mean?), Self-revelation (How am I doing in light of the truth unveiled?), and Application (Now that I know what I know, what will I do to integrate this truth into my life?). You won't be able to use all the questions in each study, but be sure to use some from each of these types of questions.

7. Connect with group members away from group time. The amount of participation you have during your group meetings is directly related to the amount of time you connect with your group members away from the meeting time.

8. Don't get impatient about the depth of relationship group members are experiencing. Building real Christian Community takes time.

9. Be sure pens and/or pencils are available for attendees at each meeting.

10. Never ask someone to pray aloud without first getting their permission.

EVERY MEETING:

1. Before the icebreakers, do not say, "Now we're going to do an icebreaker." The meeting should feel like a conversation from beginning to end, not a classroom experience.

2. Be certain every member responds to the icebreaker questions. The goal is for every person to hear his or her own voice early in the meeting. People will then feel comfortable to converse later on. If members can't think of a response, let them know you'll come back to them after the others have spoken.

3. Remember, a great group leader talks less than 10% of the time. If you ask a question and no one answers, just wait. If you create an environment where you fill the gaps of silence, the group will quickly learn they needn't join you in the conversation.

4. Don't be hesitant to call people by name as you ask them to respond to questions or to give their opinions. Be sensitive, but engage everyone in the conversation.

5. Don't ask people to read aloud unless you have gotten their permission prior to the meeting. Feel free to ask for volunteers to read.

THE GROUP

Each small group has it's own persona. Every group is made up of a unique set of personalities, backgrounds, and life experiences. This diversity creates a dynamic distinctive to that specific group of people. Embracing the unique character of your group and the individual's in that group is vital to group members experiencing all you're hoping for.

Treat each person as special, responsible, and valuable members of this Christian community. By doing so you'll bring out the best in each of them thus creating a living, breathing, life-changing group dynamic.

WHAT CAN YOU EXPECT?

Because group members are still experiencing numbness and emotions are stirring within them, at the outset, members will be on their best behavior. Most attendees will, as they understand the openness necessary and requested by the group, withdraw for at time.

Some attendees will experience fatigue which will lead to them shutting down emotionally. This is natural and is one of the things our body does to prevent emotional overload.

There are some emotions and phases unique to people dealing with loss. You need to be aware of these.

Anger – normal, but maybe difficult to express due to shame or guilt. Clearly directed in the case of a divorce or job loss. Can be turned inward (depression).

Guilt – Sometimes called the "What ifs" or the "If onlys".

Sadness – This is generally in direct proportion to the attachment to the person or object lost. The greater the loss, the deeper the sadness.

Anxiety and Helplessness - Fear of the unknown can increase anxiety.

Frustration – Adjusting to the absence of things needed and cherished is normal. Becomes a problem when there are demands to go back to the way it was

Depression – When the anger of a loss is directed inward

Loss of Identity – That which was lost is what gives some persons their sense of identity. Their self-worth is built around the job they use to have, the spouse they use to love and care for. When that thing no longer exists in their lives they find themselves without and are lost in a sea of unknown meaning.

You will be the most helpful when you focus on how the each individual is adjusting and reminding them that these emotions are normal. When short tempers, changes in physical habits, such as sleep, eating, apathy, and others appear to be long term, refer them to a pastor or competent Christian counselor. You can get a list of counselors from your pastor and other ministers.

Holidays and special occasions are especially difficult for people who are in the grief process. What was once a happy time is now brings difficulty and pain.

Places may also bring back memories that are difficult to deal with alone. If a member has an engagement in a location that would be a painful reminder of the past go with them and/or ask the group if one of them might be there for this individual. You may hear, "This is something I have to do alone." You can respect their desire to be strong, but remind them that even alone, it is God who will give them strength, and that you will pray for them.

WHAT CAN YOU DO?

Support – Provide plenty of time for support among the group members. Encourage members to connect with each other between meetings when necessary. Some examples are:
a) arranging a funeral
b) coping with the side effects of treatment,
c) how to look for a job
d) how to apply for financial assistance
e) mowing the grass
f) cleaning someone's home

Shared Feelings – Reassure the members how normal their feelings are; even if relief and sadness are mixed together. Encourage the members to share their feelings with one another.

Advice Giving – Avoid giving advice. Encourage cross-talk (members talking to each other), but limit advice giving. Should and ought to statements tend to increase the guilt the loss has already created.

Silence – Silence is not a problem. Even though it may seem awkward, silence is just a sign that people are not ready to talk. It DOES NOT mean they aren't thinking or feeling. If the silence needs to be broken, be sure you break it with the desire to move forward.

Prayer – Prayer is vital to healing. Starting and ending with prayer is important. However, people may need prayer in the middle of the session. Here's a way to know when the time is right to pray. If a member is sharing and you sense a need to pray, then begin to look for a place to add it.

Feelings vs. Right Choices and Thinking – There may be a temptation to overemphasize feelings rather that choices and thinking. It is important that you keep the focus on moving forward regardless of how we feel. Our feelings may make the journey slow, but left to feelings only, progress will shut down.

Group Reunion – As you move toward the end of the study, be aware that it is a bittersweet time for the group. It will be painful for them to say goodbye to one another. Set a time for the group to have a reunion.

Meeting Planner

The leader or facilitator of our group is _____ .

The apprentice facilitator for this group is _____ .

WE WILL MEET ON THE FOLLOWING DATES AND TIMES:

	Date	Day	Time
Session 1	_____	_____	_____
Session 2	_____	_____	_____
Session 3	_____	_____	_____
Session 4	_____	_____	_____
Session 5	_____	_____	_____
Session 6	_____	_____	_____
Session 7	_____	_____	_____
Session 8	_____	_____	_____

LOCATION WE WILL MEET AT:

Session 1 _____

Session 2 _____

Session 3 _____

Session 4 _____

Session 5 _____

Session 6 _____

Session 7 _____

Session 8 _____

REFRESHMENTS WILL BE ARRANGED BY:

Session 1 _____

Session 2 _____

Session 3 _____

Session 4 _____

Session 5 _____

Session 6 _____

Session 7 _____

Session 8 _____

CHILDCARE WILL BE ARRANGED BY:

Session 1 _____

Session 2 _____

Session 3 _____

Session 4 _____

Session 5 _____

Session 6 _____

Session 7 _____

Session 8 _____

Welcome to Community!

Meeting together with a group of people to study God's Word and experience life together is an exciting adventure.

A small group is ... *a group of people unwilling to settle for anything less than redemptive community.*

Core Values

COMMUNITY:
God is relational, so He created us to live in relationship with Him and each other. Authentic community involves sharing life together and connecting on many levels with the people in our group.

GROUP PROCESS:
Developing authentic community requires a step-by-step process. It's a journey of sharing our stories with each other and learning together.

STAGES OF DEVELOPMENT:
Every healthy group goes through various stages as it matures over a period of months or years. We begin with the birth of a new group, deepen our relationships in the growth and development stages, and ultimately multiply to form other new groups.

INTERACTIVE BIBLE STUDY:
God provided the Bible as an instruction manual of life. We need to deepen our understanding of God's Word. People learn and remember more as they wrestle with truth and learn from others. The process of Bible discovery and group interaction will enhance our growth.

EXPERIENTIAL GROWTH:

The goal of studying the Bible together is not merely a quest for knowledge, but should result in real life change. Beyond solely reading, studying, and dissecting the Bible, being a disciple of Christ involves reunifying knowledge with experience. We do this by bringing our questions to God, opening a dialogue with our hearts (instead of killing our desires), and utilizing other ways to listen to God speak to us (group interaction, nature, art, movies, circumstances, etc.). Experiential growth is always grounded in the Bible as God's primary means of revelation and our ultimate truth-source.

THE POWER OF GOD:

Our processes and strategies will be ineffective unless we invite and embrace the presence and power of God. In order to experience community and growth, Jesus needs to be the centerpiece of our group experiences and the Holy Spirit must be at work.

REDEMPTIVE COMMUNITY:

Healing occurs best within the context of community and relationships. A key aspect of our spiritual development and journey through grief and pain is seeing ourselves through the eyes of others, sharing our stories, and ultimately being set free from the secrets and lies we embrace that enslave our souls.

MISSION:

God has invited us into a larger story with a great mission. It is a mission that involves setting captives free and healing the broken-hearted (Isaiah 61:1-2). However, we can only join in this mission to the degree that we've let Jesus bind up our wounds and set us free. As a group experiences true redemptive community, other people will be attracted to that group, and through that group to Jesus. We should be alert to other people that we can invite when a new group is getting ready to start up.

Stages of Group Life

Each healthy small group will move through various stages as it matures. There is no prescribed time frame for moving through these stages because each group is unique.

BIRTH STAGE: This is the time in which group members form relationships and begin to develop community.

MULTIPLY STAGE: The group begins the multiplication process. Members pray about their involvement in establishing new groups. The new groups begin the cycle again with the Birth Stage.

GROWTH STAGE: Here the group members begin to care for one another as they learn what it means to apply what they have discovered through Bible study, shared experiences, worship, and prayer

DEVELOP STAGE: The Bible study and shared experiences deepen while the group members develop their gifts and skills. The group explores ways to invite neighbors, friends, and coworkers to meetings.

SUBGROUPING: If you have more than 12 people at a meeting, Serendipity House recommends dividing into smaller subgroups after the "Breaking the Ice" segment. Ask one person to be the leader of each subgroup, following the "Leader" directions for the session. The Group Leader should bring the subgroups back together for the closing. Subgrouping is also very useful when more openness and intimacy is required. The "Connecting" segment in each session is a great time to divide into smaller groups of 4 to 6 people.

SHARING YOUR STORIES

The sessions in *Recovering from Divorce* are designed to help you share some of your personal lives with the people in your group as you learn to walk through your grief and embrace God's hope. Through your time together, each member of the group is encouraged to move from low risk, less personal sharing to higher risk communication. Real community will not develop apart from increasing intimacy over time.

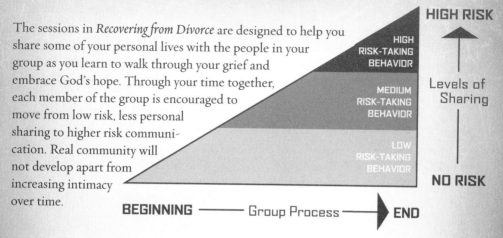

SHARING YOUR LIVES

As you share your lives together during this time, it is important to recognize that it is God who has brought each person to this group, gifting the individuals to play a vital role in the group (1 Corinthians 12:1). Each of you was uniquely designed to contribute in your own unique way to building into the lives of the other people in your group. As you get to know one another better, consider the following four areas that will be unique for each person. These areas will help you get a "grip" how you can better support others and how they can support you.

G – SPIRITUAL GIFTS: God has given you unique spiritual gifts
(1 Corinthians 12; Romans 12:3-8; Ephesians 4:1-16; etc.)

R – RESOURCES: You have resources that perhaps only you can share, including skill, abilities, possessions, money, and time
(Acts 2:44-47; Ecclesiastes 4:9-12, etc.)

I – INDIVIDUAL EXPERIENCES: You have past experiences, both good and bad, that God can use to strengthen others
(2 Corinthians 1:3-7; Romans 8:28, etc.)

P – PASSIONS: There are things that excite and motivate you. God has given you those desires and passions to use for His purposes
(Psalm 37:4,23; Proverbs 3:5-6,13-18; etc.)

To better understand how a group should function and develop in these four areas, consider going through the Serendipity study entitled *Great Beginnings*.

About the Author

Ramon Presson, a clinically certified marriage and family therapist, has served as an assistant pastor and counselor for almost two decades. He is the founder of LifeChange Counseling and Coaching in Franklin, Tennessee.

Presson is the creator and co-author with Dr. Gary Chapman of both *Love Talks for Couples* and *Love Talks for Families.* He has also written three additional Serendipity House studies: *Vital Pursuits; Intentional Choices;* and *Radical Reconciliation.*

He has written articles for *Marriage Partnership, Discipleship Journal, Christian Single,* and is a frequent writer for *Single Adult Ministry Journal.*

Ramon lives with his wife and two sons in Thompson Station, Tennessee.

For more information about Ramon Presson or LifeChange, visit www.ramonpresson.com.

Acknowledgments

This project was a true team effort. We wish to thank the team that labored to make this life-changing small-group experience a reality.

Special thanks to Ramon Presson for writing this excellent resource.

Publisher: Ron Keck

Editorial team: Ben Colter, Ron Keck, Rick Howerton, and Lori Mayes

Art direction: Scott Lee of Scott Lee Designs

Cover design: Roy Roper of Wideyedesign

Interior design and production: Scott Lee and Brian Marschall

Real Help for Real People Living Real Life.

Designed for Support Groups, Recovery Groups, Small Groups,
Men's & Women's Accountability Groups, and Church Classes

Honest, experiential Bible study series addressing the storms in life
and how to make it through them

Cultivates a sense of redemptive community at a time when
the urge to detach and live in isolation is strong

Experience Restoration

Another Picking Up the Pieces resource,
*Pursued By God – An Experience in Redemptive
Worship CD,* can encourage you on your journey
to freedom. Engage your soul at the deepest
level through songs of redemptive worship—
worship as it was meant to be … real-time,
multidirectional, intimate interaction with
God Himself. It provides an opportunity to
experience healing that can only come when
we share our heart with God, and listen for
what He wants to say to us personally.

Available from
Serendipity
House

GROUP DIRECTORY

Write your name on this page. Pass your books around and ask your group members to fill in their names and contact information in each other's books.

Your Name: _____

Name: _____	Name: _____
Address: _____	Address: _____
City: _____	City: _____
Zip Code: _____	Zip Code: _____
Home Phone: _____	Home Phone: _____
Mobile Phone: _____	Mobile Phone: _____
E-mail: _____	E-mail: _____

Name: _____
Address: _____
City: _____
Zip Code: _____
Home Phone: _____
Mobile Phone: _____
E-mail: _____

Name: _____
Address: _____
City: _____
Zip Code: _____
Home Phone: _____
Mobile Phone: _____
E-mail: _____

Name: _____
Address: _____
City: _____
Zip Code: _____
Home Phone: _____
Mobile Phone: _____
E-mail: _____

Name: _____
Address: _____
City: _____
Zip Code: _____
Home Phone: _____
Mobile Phone: _____
E-mail: _____

Name: _____
Address: _____
City: _____
Zip Code: _____
Home Phone: _____
Mobile Phone: _____
E-mail: _____

Name: _____
Address: _____
City: _____
Zip Code: _____
Home Phone: _____
Mobile Phone: _____
E-mail: _____

Name: _____
Address: _____
City: _____
Zip Code: _____
Home Phone: _____
Mobile Phone: _____
E-mail: _____

Name: _____
Address: _____
City: _____
Zip Code: _____
Home Phone: _____
Mobile Phone: _____
E-mail: _____

Name: _____   Name: _____
Address: _____   Address: _____
City: _____   City: _____
Zip Code: _____   Zip Code: _____
Home Phone: _____   Home Phone: _____
Mobile Phone: _____   Mobile Phone: _____
E-mail: _____   E-mail: _____

Name: _____   Name: _____
Address: _____   Address: _____
City: _____   City: _____
Zip Code: _____   Zip Code: _____
Home Phone: _____   Home Phone: _____
Mobile Phone: _____   Mobile Phone: _____
E-mail: _____   E-mail: _____

Name: _____   Name: _____
Address: _____   Address: _____
City: _____   City: _____
Zip Code: _____   Zip Code: _____
Home Phone: _____   Home Phone: _____
Mobile Phone: _____   Mobile Phone: _____
E-mail: _____   E-mail: _____

Name: _____   Name: _____
Address: _____   Address: _____
City: _____   City: _____
Zip Code: _____   Zip Code: _____
Home Phone: _____   Home Phone: _____
Mobile Phone: _____   Mobile Phone: _____
E-mail: _____   E-mail: _____

Name: _____   Name: _____
Address: _____   Address: _____
City: _____   City: _____
Zip Code: _____   Zip Code: _____
Home Phone: _____   Home Phone: _____
Mobile Phone: _____   Mobile Phone: _____
E-mail: _____   E-mail: _____